Immortality

Basic Problems in Philosophy Series

A. I. Melden and Stanley Munsat
University of California, Irvine
General Editors

The Problem of Abortion
Joel Feinberg, Rockefeller University

Ethical Relativism
John Ladd, Brown University

Human Rights
A. I. Melden

Egoism and Altruism
Ronald D. Milo, University of Arizona

Guilt and Shame
Herbert Morris, University of California, Los Angeles

The Analytic-Synthetic Distinction
Stanley Munsat

Civil Disobedience and Violence
Jeffrie G. Murphy, University of Arizona

Punishment and Rehabilitation
Jeffrie G. Murphy

Immortality
Terence Penelhum, University of Calgary

Morality and the Law
Richard A. Wasserstrom, University of California, Los Angeles

War and Morality
Richard A. Wasserstrom

Immortality

edited by

Terence Penelhum
The University of Calgary

Wadsworth Publishing Company, Inc.
Belmont, California

TO EDITH

236.22
P37

Cover: Russ K. Leong

Terence Penelhum is Professor of Philosophy and Religious Studies at The University of Calgary, where he has
also served as Head of the Philosophy (1963-70) Department
and Dean of Arts and Science (1964-67). He obtained the
M.A. from the University of Edinburgh and the B.Phil. from
Oxford, and has contributed numerous articles to philosophical journals. He is author of *Survival and Disembodied
Existence* (1970), *Religion and Rationality* (1971), and
Problems of Religious Knowledge (1971). He is also
co-editor, with J. J. MacIntosh, of *The First Critique*
(Wadsworth 1969).

ISBN 0-534-00333-8
L.C. Cat. Card No. 73-88463
Printed in the United States of America

1 2 3 4 5 6 7 8 9 10—77 76 75 74 73

To keep the price of this book as low as possible, we have
used an economical means of typesetting. We welcome your
comments.

Series Foreword

The Basic Problems in Philosophy Series is designed to meet the need of students and teachers of philosophy, mainly but not exclusively at the undergraduate level, for collections of essays devoted to some fairly specific philosophical problems.

In recent years there have been numerous paperback collections on a variety of philosophical topics. Those teachers who wish to refer their students to a set of essays on a specific philosophical problem have usually been frustrated, however, since most of these collections range over a wide set of issues and problems. The present series attempts to remedy this situation by presenting together, within each volume, key writings on a single philosophical issue.

Given the magnitude of the literature, there can be no thought of completeness. Rather, the materials included are those that, in the judgment of the editor, must be mastered first by the student who wishes to acquaint himself with relevant issues and their ramifications. To this end, historical as well as contemporary writings are included.

Each volume in the series contains an introduction by the editor to set the stage for the arguments contained in the essays and a bibliography to help the student who wishes to pursue the topic at a more advanced level.

A. I. Melden
S. Munsat

Contents

Introduction   1

Part One   The Immortality of the Soul

Immortality   11
Peter Geach

Survival and the Idea of "Another World"   21
H. H. Price

Part Two   The Resurrection of the Body

The Resurrection of Christ and the
Resurrection of Men   51
St. Paul

Immortality of the Soul or Resurrection
of the Dead?   53
Oscar Cullmann

from "Theology and Verification"   86
John Hick

The Resurrection: Objections and Answers   92
St. Thomas Aquinas

Part Three   The Evidence of Psychical Research

The Problem of Life After Death   103
H. H. Price

The Question of Survival   118
Antony Flew

Part Four   Religious Belief and the Afterlife

             Towards a Christian Theology of Death   141
             John Hick

Bibliography   159

Introduction

Millions of people throughout recorded history have believed in a life after death. In spite of the secularization of our present age, millions still do. Those who do not believe in it are apt to think that those who do are indulging in wishful thinking. No doubt some of them are, but it is also common for men to think of a hereafter with fear, rather than with hope. Consider Hamlet:

> . . . who would fardels bear,
> To grunt and sweat under a weary life,
> But that the dread of something after death,
> The undiscover'd country from whose bourn
> No traveller returns, puzzles the will,
> And makes us rather bear those ills we have
> Than fly to others that we know not of?[1]

Indeed, what is called fear of death may often be fear of what might follow it. Some think this fear is spiritually healthy—that it makes us, like Hamlet, reject suicide as an escape and conduct ourselves better for fear of judgment hereafter. Viewed in this light, it is skepticism, rather than belief, that is due to wishful thinking.

The writings in this book deal only indirectly with the motives men have for believing or disbelieving in an afterlife. They are more specifically concerned with clarifying the meaning of this belief and with the question of its truth or falsity. These questions cannot be separated. It is possible that even a belief as widespread and familiar as this is so confused that a careful analysis of it would reveal that it cannot be expressed coherently. In

---

[1]*Hamlet*, Act III, Scene I.

that event, it could not possibly be true—or straightforwardly false either. So one of the questions our writers ask (especially Flew, Geach, Hick, and Price) is: Can a belief in survival after death be expressed coherently or not? The reader who finds this question surprising will find that these writers' contributions make it very clear why it has been asked, whether or not they answer it satisfactorily. As soon as we attempt to confront this question, however, we are faced with the fact that the belief has been expressed in many forms, some of which may contain confusions and others not. The two versions discussed here are the belief in the immortality of the soul and the belief in bodily resurrection.

The doctrine of the immortality of the soul is the doctrine that a person survives death in an immaterial form. ("Form" here cannot, of course, mean "shape.") On this view, only the body dies; and when it does, the soul, or spirit, separates from it to live on, disembodied. Many of those who believe there is an afterlife would unhesitatingly identify the doctrine of the immortality of the soul as the version of this belief which they espouse. It has two important implications. First, it implies the dualistic view that people are composite beings, consisting of an immaterial soul and a physical body. Second, it implies that the immaterial soul is the real person, and the body is merely his temporary residence. This second implication is critically important, for if someone held that the soul survived the death of the body but did not identify the soul with the real person, he would not believe that the *person* survived the body's death; for him, the soul that continued would merely be a bundle of spiritual *remains*. We seem to find such a view in Homer; his gloomy view of the plight of the shades in Hades is the result of the assumption that they are only the subpersonal relics of organisms that have died.[2]

In sharp contrast, the doctrine of bodily resurrection is the doctrine that what will live on, at least in the final outcome, will be the physically re-created human person rather than an immaterial soul. This doctrine seems to be the only possible form of belief in survival for anyone who denies the dualistic view of the nature of human personality. In view of the familiar fact that human bodies

---

[2]On this and other historical references, the reader is referred to the Bibliography at the end of this volume.

disintegrate after death, the expectation of a resurrection is the expectation of a *miraculous* future act of God.

So it is no logical accident that the belief in immortality is held by thinkers who consider that eternal life belongs to the essence of the soul and that the temporal restrictions of the body are alien to it; and it is no logical accident that belief in resurrection is found among those who think of eternal life as a gift rather than a right. The nature of the intellectual and religious environments of these two beliefs is the central topic of the article by Oscar Cullmann. He claims that the doctrine of immortality is not, as many have assumed, a Christian belief at all. It is well known that its most eloquent expression in Western literature is in Plato's *Phaedo*. Plato there represents Socrates as arguing for the soul's permanence and supreme value in a way designed to supersede the Homeric tradition. It has commonly been taken for granted that the views Socrates proclaims can be Christianized by simply denying his claim that the soul exists before it enters the body (which the most impressive arguments of the dialogue are supposed to prove) and retaining merely his conviction that it lives on after the body dies. Cullmann challenges this assumption by insisting that the primitive (that is, original) Christian doctrine is that of resurrection, which entails a totally different understanding of life and death from that expressed in the Platonic tradition. Cullmann's arguments have been challenged, but there is no better way to begin reflection on the religious place of the belief in an afterlife than by considering them.

The writings in this volume will be concerned only with those survival doctrines that are found (rightfully or not) within the Christian tradition and in Judaism and Islam. Whatever their differences, these doctrines all envision an individual, personal, and unique form of survival. It is proclaimed and expected that all or some persons will live again after death, either immediately or at some future time of consummation; that each person who survives, survives as a personal being; that each person who survives has one and only one postmortem life that is usually thought to be eternal and does not return for another life-span in another human body; and that each postmortem person is identical with one, and only one, person who has passed through this life, however much transformed by the passage from this life to the next.

These doctrines differ radically from the doctrines of reincarnation that are asserted, or presupposed, in the Hindu and Buddhist religious traditions. These traditions require separate and detailed study, and while some of the problems dealt with here are undoubtedly relevant to such a study, the coherence of this volume would have been destroyed by any attempt to embark upon it. This problem can easily be seen when we reflect that the cycle of incarnations is not confined to human or personal lives, and that the goal of the spiritual disciplines associated with these traditions is usually said to be liberation *from*, not *into*, individual personal existence.

If we wish to understand the meaning of beliefs in life after death, we must enquire into the nature of their religious connections, for these affect the forms in which the beliefs are presented. But the two main beliefs raise basic and intricate conceptual issues in epistemology and the philosophy of mind as well; and these issues must be confronted when we ask whether either form of belief can be coherently expressed.

What is said to live on after death is a *person*. If so, then the form of life the postmortem being takes must be a form that is logically possible for a person to have. But what if activities *essential to being a person* are inconceivable in the postmortem state? This possibility is most obviously a problem for those who believe in disembodied survival; for a disembodied person is body-less. Could a disembodied person see (in the absence of eyes); or communicate (in the absence of organs of speech or hearing); or act (in the absence of limbs); or think (in the absence of a brain or nervous system)? The question in each case is a logical one: can one assert that such an activity takes place without contradicting the assumption that the being it is ascribed to has no body? It is not a question about whether, in this life, these activities take place without bodily performances, for most would agree that they do not, but rather a question about whether we can talk without contradiction of another world in which they do. If we cannot talk about such a world, then perhaps the very concept of disembodied personal existence is incoherent. Flew raises this challenge most pointedly, and Price attempts to meet it in his "Survival and the Idea of 'Another World.'" Price argues that a disembodied person could create for himself a psychical counterpart of the flesh-and-blood personal existence he knew before death.

On the face of it, this problem only seems to arise for someone who believes in resurrection if he insists too unwisely on the degree to which the body of the resurrection is transformed. Obviously, St. Paul, in the famous and normative passage from his First Letter to the Corinthians, insisted upon it, but perhaps not to the extent

that it raises *this* problem. On this matter each reader
must be his own judge.

A problem that neither view can avoid is the problem
of identity. What can entitle us to say that the being who
continues after a person's death is identical with that person? This problem is raised by Geach and by Flew in considering the doctrine of immortality. In daily life we usually identify people we meet as people we knew before by
their physical characteristics. If this is not possible,
we may resort to tests of memory. Philosophers disagree
over whether the "physical" criterion of bodily identity is
a more fundamental standard of personal identity than the
"mental" criterion of memory. We do not have to decide
such a question in daily life, but in reflecting on the
possibility of survival we cannot escape so easily. For if
the physical criterion is fundamental, then its obvious
absence creates a critical difficulty for the doctrine of
immortality. If possession of the same physical body makes
a person at one time the same as a person at another, then
no disembodied person can be identified with a previously
embodied one, and there is an obvious problem in claiming
that the disembodied person itself can persist through time.

Perhaps one can resort to memory here also. Perhaps
what makes the disembodied spirit the same as a previously
embodied person is the fact that the spirit remembers experiences in the embodied person's life? However, there is
a problem here in that only real memories, and not apparent
ones, can be appealed to; but one of the essential differences between a real memory and an apparent one is that in
real memory the later recollection is not only a recollection of something that really happened, but is of something
that really happened to the person recalling it. But to
concede this fact is to bring in once again some standard
of identity other than memory; and the obvious standard,
bodily identity, is not available.

But does not the doctrine of resurrection once again,
escape this difficulty? Would the resurrectee not have the
same body as his predecessor? Unfortunately, these things
are not so clear. A critic can easily suggest that what
will rise in the future is not the very same person, in the
very same body, but merely a replica of him. However many
accurate recollections the resurrectee will have, however
much he may feel guilt or pride about the doings of the man
who died, the fact that the body which died may have been
destroyed makes it just as correct to say that the resurrection body is a new (and perhaps superior) duplicate of
it as to say that it is numerically the same. And if their
bodies are not the same, how can we say with confidence

that *they* are? (The natural move here is to reintroduce
the belief in disembodied survival in order to bridge the
gap between death and resurrection and thereby certify the
identity. But to do this is to add the problems of the belief in disembodied survival to those one has already.)
John Hick tries to meet these logical difficulties in his
comments on resurrection, and in the two chapters included
here from the *Summa Contra Gentiles* St. Thomas Aquinas describes and attempts to refute earlier versions of these
same problems.

These are the logical difficulties some have found in
the belief in a life after death. But many ask for more
than a mere resolution of these issues before they will
listen seriously to a doctrine of such importance. They
want to know whether, when we know so much about the depend-
ence of mental life in this world upon the state of the
body, there is any positive evidence that any human personality *has* ever lived on after death. Of course, no present
evidence could guarantee *eternal* survival or guarantee a
resurrection in the future, and if we turn to empirical
evidence there is the risk that it might support an unortho-
dox belief in survival rather than an orthodox one. But
there have been, over the centuries, many alleged evidences
of the persistence of human personality after death, and it
is absurd not to pay attention to them. In "The Problem of
Life After Death," Professor H. H. Price offers his esti-
mate of some of this evidence, especially that collected
through observation of mediums who claim to be in communication with the dead. It is striking that when the hypothesis of survival seems the only reasonable alternative,
many who do not wish to accept it will cheerfully postulate
other paranormal processes such as telepathy or clairvoyance, which they would resolutely refuse to consider as explanatory possibilities in other contexts. Price discusses
the plausibility of these alternatives, and his assessment
of this material should be compared with that of Antony
Flew, who believes that the survival explanation entails
far greater complexities. These two discussions are an excellent introduction to the extensive, baffling, and perhaps important literature of psychical research.

Most who accept the belief in survival, however, do
so not because of the evidence of mediums but as a part of
a personal commitment to the religious traditions encom-
passing the belief. In recent years, there have been widely publicized attempts to de-supernaturalize these traditions. The doctrine of survival has been reinterpreted, or
dropped, in the interest of retaining what are considered
to be more central religious doctrines in a secular age.

These attempts may be true to religious essentials, or they may not. Both those who belong to these traditions and those outside them have an interest in deciding this. The skeptic is well-advised to be accurate in his understanding of what he rejects, just as the believer is to be accurate in his understanding of what he believes. For this reason, John Hick's theological assessment of the place of the belief in an afterlife in the Christian tradition is of general concern. It serves as a reminder that when we discuss life after death, we are not only examining some of the most widespread and basic human hopes and fears but also examining a question in which the concerns of philosophical, religious, and historical thought cannot help coming together.

Part One The Immortality of the Soul

IMMORTALITY

Peter Geach

Everybody knows that men die, and though most of us have read the advertisement 'Millions now living will never die,' it is commonly believed that every man born will some day die; yet historically many men have believed that there is a life after death, and indeed that this after-life will never end. That is: there has been a common belief both in *survival* of bodily death and in *immortality*. Now a philosopher might interest himself specially in immortality, as opposed to survival; conceding survival for the sake of argument, he might raise and examine conceptual difficulties about *endless* survival. But the question of immortality cannot even arise unless men do survive bodily death; and, as we shall see, there are formidable difficulties even about survival. It is these difficulties I shall be discussing, not the special ones about endless survival.

There are various views as to the character of the after-life. One view is that man has a subtle, ordinarily invisible, body which survives the death of the ordinary gross body. This view has a long history, and seems to be quite popular in England at the moment. So far as I can see, the view is open to no philosophical objection, but likewise wholly devoid of philosophical interest; the mind-body problem must after all be just the same for an ethereal body as for a gross one. There could clearly be no philosophical reasons for belief in such subtle bodies, but only empirical ones; such reasons are in fact alleged, and we are urged to study the evidence.

Peter Geach is Professor of Logic at the University of Leeds. His writings include *Mental Acts* (1957), *Reference and Generality* (1969), and (with G.E.M. Anscombe) *Three Philosophers* (1961). This essay appeared in the volume *God and the Soul*, by Peter Geach, copyright © 1969 by Peter Geach, published by Routledge and Kegan Paul, London, and Schocken Books Inc., New York, in 1969. It is reprinted here by permission of the author and publishers.

Philosophy can at this point say something: about what sort of evidence would be required. The existence of subtle bodies is a matter within the purview of physical science; evidence for it should satisfy such criteria of existence as physicists use, and should refer not only to what people say they have seen, heard, and felt, but also to effects produced by subtle bodies on physicists' apparatus. The believer in 'subtle bodies' must, I think, accept the physicist's criteria of existence; there would surely be a conceptual muddle in speaking of 'bodies' but saying they might be incapable of affecting any physical apparatus. For what distinguishes real physical objects from hallucinations, even collective hallucinations, is that physical objects act on one another, and do so in just the same way whether they are being observed or not; this is the point, I think, at which a phenomenalist account of physical objects breaks down. If, therefore, 'subtle bodies' produce no physical effects, they are not bodies at all.

How is it, then, that 'subtle bodies' have never forced themselves upon the attention of physicists, as X-rays did, by spontaneous interference with physical apparatus? There are supposed to be a lot of 'subtle bodies' around, and physicists have a lot of delicate apparatus; yet physicists not engaged in psychical research are never bothered by the interference of 'subtle bodies'. In these circumstances I think it wholly irrational to believe in 'subtle bodies'. Moreover, when I who am no physicist am invited to study the evidence for 'subtle bodies', I find that very fact suspicious. The discoverers of X-rays and electrons did not appeal to the lay public, but to physicists, to study the evidence; and so long as physicists (at least in general) refuse to take 'subtle bodies' seriously, a study of evidence for them by a layman like myself would be a waste of time.

When *philosophers* talk of life after death, what they mostly have in mind is a doctrine that may be called Platonic—it is found in its essentials in the *Phaedo*. It may be briefly stated thus: 'Each man's make-up includes a wholly immaterial thing, his mind and soul. It is the mind that sees and hears and feels and thinks and chooses—in a word, is conscious. The mind is the person; the body is extrinsic to the person, like a suit of clothes. Though body and mind affect one another, the mind's existence is quite independent of the body's; and there is thus no reason why the mind should not go on being conscious indefinitely after the death of the body, and even if it never again has with any body that sort of connexion which it now has.'

This Platonic doctrine has a strong appeal, and there are plausible arguments in its favour. It appears a clearly intelligible supposition that I should go on after death having the same sorts of experience as I now have, even if I then have no body at all. For although these experiences are connected with processes in the body—sight, for example, with processes in the eyes, optic nerves, and brain—nevertheless there is no necessity of thought about the connexion—it is easy to conceive of someone who has no eyes having the experience called sight. He would be having the same experience as I who have eyes do, and I know what sort of experience that is because I have the experience.

Let us now examine these arguments. When a word can be used to stand for a private experience, like the words 'seeing' or 'pain', it is certainly tempting to suppose that giving these words a meaning is itself a private experience—indeed that they get their meaning just from the experiences they stand for. But this is really nonsense: if a sentence I hear or utter contains the word 'pain', do I help myself to grasp its sense by giving myself a pain? Might not this be, on the contrary, rather distracting? As Wittgenstein said, to think you get the concept of pain by having a pain is like thinking you get the concept of a minus quantity by running up an overdraft. Our concepts of seeing, hearing, pain, anger, etc., apply in the first instance to human beings; we willingly extend them (say) to cats, dogs, and horses, but we rightly feel uncomfortable about extending them to very alien creatures and speaking of a slug's hearing or an angry ant. Do we know at all what it would be to apply such concepts to an immaterial being? I think not.

One may indeed be tempted to evade difficulties by saying: 'An immaterial spirit is angry or in pain if it feels *the same way* as I do when I am angry or in pain'. But, as Wittgenstein remarked, this is just like saying: 'Of course I know what it is for the time on the Sun to be five o'clock: it's five o'clock on the Sun at the very moment when it's five o'clock here!'—which plainly gets us no forrader. If there is a difficulty in passing from 'I am in pain' or 'Smith is in pain' to 'an immaterial spirit is in pain', there is equally a difficulty in passing from 'Smith feels the same way as I do' to 'an immaterial spirit feels the same way as I do'.

In fact, the question is, whether a private experience does suffice, as is here supposed, to give a meaning to a psychological verb like 'to see'. I am not trying to throw doubt on there being private experiences; of course men have thoughts they do not utter and pains they do not show; of course I may see something without any behaviour to show

I see it; nor do I mean to emasculate these propositions with neo-behaviourist dialectics. But it is not a question of whether seeing is (sometimes) a private experience, but whether one can attach meaning to the verb 'to see' by a private uncheckable performance; and this is what I maintain one cannot do to any word at all.

One way to show that a word's being given a meaning cannot be a private uncheckable performance is the following: We can take a man's word for it that a linguistic expression has given him some private experience—e.g. has revived a painful memory, evoked a visual image, or given him a thrill in the pit of the stomach. But we cannot take his word for it that he attached a sense to the expression, even if we accept his *bona fides*; for later events may convince us that in fact he attached no sense to the expression. Attaching sense to an expression is thus not to be identified with any private experience that accompanies the expression; and I have argued this, not by attacking the idea of private experiences, but by contrasting the attaching of sense to an expression with some typical private experiences that may be connected with the expression.

We give words a sense—whether they are psychological words like 'seeing' and 'pain,' or other words—by getting into a way of using them; and though a man can invent for himself a way of using a word, it must be a way that other people *could* follow—otherwise we are back to the idea of conferring meaning by a private uncheckable performance. Well, how do we eventually use such words as 'see,' 'hear,' 'feel,' when we have got into the way of using them? We do not exercise these concepts only so as to pick our cases of seeing and the rest in our separate worlds of sense-experience; on the contrary, these concepts are used in association with a host of other concepts relating, e.g., to the physical characteristics of what is seen and the behaviour of those who do see. In saying this I am not putting forward a theory, but just reminding you of very familiar features in the everyday use of the verb 'to see' and related expressions; our ordinary talk about seeing would cease to be intelligible if there were cut out of it such expressions as 'I can't see, it's too far off', 'I caught his eye', 'Don't look round', etc. Do not let the bogy of behaviourism scare you off observing these features; I am not asking you to believe that 'to see' is itself a word for a kind of behaviour. But the concept of seeing can be maintained only because it has threads of connexion with these other non-psychological concepts; break enough threads, and the concept of seeing collapses.

We can now see the sort of difficulties that arise if
we try to apply concepts like *seeing* and *feeling* to disembodied spirits. Let me give an actual case of a psychological concept's collapsing when its connexions were broken.
Certain hysterics claimed to have a magnetic sense; it was
discovered, however, that their claim to be having magnetic
sensations did not go with the actual presence of a magnet
in their environment, but only with their belief that a
magnet was present. Psychologists did not then take the
line: We may take the patients' word for it that they have
peculiar sensations—only the term 'magnetic sensations'
has proved inappropriate, as having been based on a wrong
causal hypothesis. On the contrary, patients' reports of
magnetic sensations were thenceforward written off as being
among the odd things that hysterical patients sometimes say.
Now far fewer of the ordinary connexions of a sensation-
concept were broken here than would be broken if we tried
to apply a sensation-concept like seeing to a disembodied
spirit.

If we conclude that the ascription of sensations and
feelings to a disembodied spirit does not make sense, it
does not obviously follow, as you might think, that we must
deny the possibility of disembodied spirits altogether.
Aquinas for example was convinced that there are disembodied
spirits but ones that cannot see or hear or feel pain or
fear or anger; he allowed them no mental operations except
those of thought and will. Damned spirits would suffer
from frustration of their evil will, but not from aches and
pains or foul odours or the like. It would take me too far
to discuss whether his reasons for thinking this were good;
I want to show what follows from this view. In our human
life thinking and choosing are intricately bound up with a
play of sensations and mental images and emotions; if after
a lifetime of thinking and choosing in this human way there
is left only a disembodied mind whose thought is wholly non-
sensuous and whose rational choices are unaccompanied by
any human feelings—can we still say there remains the same
person? Surely not: such a soul is not the person who died
but a mere remnant of him. And this is just what Aquinas
says (in his commentary on I Corinthians 15): *anima mea non
est ego*, my soul is not I; and if only souls are saved, *I*
am not saved, nor is any man. If some time after Peter
Geach's death there is again a man identifiable as Peter
Geach, then Peter Geach again, or still, lives: otherwise
not.

Though a surviving mental remnant of a person, pre-
serving some sort of physical continuity with the man you

knew, would not be Peter Geach, this does not show that
such a measure of survival is not possible; but its possibility does raise serious difficulties, even if such dehu-
manized thinking and willing are really conceivable at all.
For *whose* thinking would this be? Could we tell whether
one or *many* disembodied spirits thought the thoughts in
question? We touch here on the old problem: what constitutes there being two disembodied minds (at the same time,
that is)? Well, what constitutes there being two pennies?
It may happen that one penny is bent and corroded while another is in mint condition; but such differences cannot be
what make the two pennies to be two—the two pennies could
not have these varied fortunes if they were not already distinct. In the same way, differences of memories or of aims
could not constitute the difference between two disembodied
minds, but could only supervene upon a difference already
existing. What does constitute the difference between two
disembodied human minds? If we could find no ground of
differentiation, then not only would that which survived
be a mere remnant of a person—there would not even be a
surviving individuality.

Could we say that souls are different because in the
first instance they were souls of different bodies, and
then remain different on that account when they are no
longer embodied? I do not think this solution would do at
all if differentiation by reference to different bodies
were merely retrospective. It might be otherwise if we
held, with Aquinas, that the relation to a body was not
merely retrospective—that each disembodied human soul permanently retained a capacity for reunion to such a body as
would reconstitute a man identifiable with the man who
died. This might satisfactorily account for the individuation of disembodied human souls; they would differ by being fitted for reunion to different bodies; but it would
entail that the possibility of disembodied human souls
stood or fell with the *possibility* of a dead man's living
again *as a man*.

Some Scholastics held that just as two pennies or two
cats differ by being different bits of matter, so human
souls differ by containing different 'spiritual matter'.
Aquinas regarded this idea as self-contradictory; it is at
any rate much too obscure to count as establishing a possibility of distinct disembodied souls. Now this recourse to
'spiritual matter' might well strike us merely as the fill-
ing of a conceptual lacuna with a nonsensical piece of jar-
gon. But it is not only Scholastic philosophers who assim-
ilate mental processes to physical ones, only thinking of
mental processes as taking place in an *immaterial* medium;

and many people think it easy to conceive of distinct disembodied souls because they are illegitimately ascribing to
souls a sort of differentiation—say, by existing *side by
side*—that can be significantly ascribed only to bodies.
The same goes for people who talk about souls as being
'fused' or 'merged' in a Great Soul; they are imagining
some such change in the world of souls as occurs to a drop
of water falling into a pool or to a small lump of wax that
is rubbed into a big one. Now if only people *talked* about
'spiritual matter', instead of just thinking in terms of it
unawares, their muddle could be more easily detected and
treated.

To sum up what I have said so far: The possibility of
life after death for Peter Geach appears to stand or fall
with the possibility of there being once again a man identifiable as Peter Geach. The existence of a disembodied soul
would not be a survival of the person Peter Geach; and even
in such a truncated form, individual existence seems to require at least a persistent possibility of the soul's again
entering into the make-up of a man who is identifiably Peter
Geach.

This suggests a form of belief in survival that seems
to have become quite popular of late in the West—at any
rate as a half-belief—namely, the belief in reincarnation.
Could it in fact have a clear sense to say that a baby born
in Oxford this year is Hitler living again?

How could it be shown that the Oxford baby was Hitler?
Presumably by memories and similarities of character. I
maintain that no amount of such evidence would make it reasonable to identify the baby as Hitler. Similarities of
character are of themselves obviously insufficient. As regards memories: If on growing up the Oxford baby reveals
knowledge of what we should ordinarily say only Hitler can
have known, does this establish a presumption that the
child is Hitler? Not at all. In normal circumstances we
know when to say 'only he can have known that'; when queer
things start happening, we have no right to stick to our
ordinary assumptions as to what can be known. And suppose
that for some time the child 'is' Hitler by our criteria,
and later on 'is' Goering? Or might not several children
simultaneously satisfy the criteria for 'being' Hitler?

These are not merely captious theoretical objections.
Spirit-mediums, we are told, will in trance convincingly
enact the part of various people: sometimes of fictitious
characters, like Martians, or Red Indians ignorant of Red
Indian languages, or the departed 'spirits' of Johnny
Walker and John Jamieson; there are even stories of mediums
giving convincing 'messages' from people who were alive and

normally conscious at the time of the 'message'. Now a medium giving messages from the dead is not said to be the dead man, but rather to be controlled by his spirit. What then can show whether the Oxford child 'is' Hitler or is merely 'controlled' by Hitler's spirit? For all these reasons the appearance that there might be good evidence for reincarnation dissolves on a closer view.

Nor do I see, for that matter, how the mental phenomena of mediumship could ever make it reasonable to believe that a human soul survived and communicated. For someone to carry on in a dramatic way quite out of his normal character is a common hysterical symptom; so if a medium does this in a trance, it is no evidence of anything except an abnormal condition of the medium's own mind. As for the medium's telling us things that 'only the dead can have known', I repeat that in these queer cases we have no right to stick to our ordinary assumptions about what can be known. Moreover, as I said, there are cases, as well-authenticated as any, in which the medium convincingly enacted the part of X and told things that 'Only X could have known' when X was in fact alive and normally conscious, so that his soul was certainly not trying to communicate by way of the medium! Even if we accept all the queer stories of spirit-messages, the result is only to open up a vast field of queer possibilities—not in the least to force us to say that mediums were possessed by such-and-such souls. This was argued by Bradley long ago in his essay 'The Evidences of Spiritualism', and he has never been answered.

How could a living man be rightly identifiable with a man who previously died? Let us first consider our normal criteria of personal identity. When we say an old man is the same person as the baby born seventy years before, we believe that the old man has material continuity with the baby. Of course this is not a criterion in the sense of being what we judge identity by; for the old man will not have been watched for seventy years continuously, even by rota! But something we regarded as disproving the material continuity (e.g. absence of a birthmark, different fingerprints) would disprove personal identity. Further, we believe that material continuity establishes a one-one relation: one baby grows up into one old man, and one old man has grown out of one baby. (Otherwise there would have to be at some stage a drastic change, a fusion or fission, which we should regard as destroying personal identity.) Moreover, the baby-body never coexists with the aged body, but develops into it.

Now, it seems to me that we cannot rightly identify a man living 'again' with a man who died unless *material* conditions of identity are fulfilled. There must be some one-one relation of material continuity between the old body and the new. I am not saying that the new body need be even in part materially *identical* with the old; this, unlike material continuity, is not required for personal identity, for the old man need not have kept even a grain of matter from the baby of seventy years ago.

We must here notice an important fallacy. I was indicating just now that I favour Aquinas's doctrine that two coexisting souls differ by being related to two different bodies and that two coexisting human bodies, like two pennies or two cats, differ by being different bits of matter. Well, if it is difference of matter that makes two bodies different, it may seem to follow that a body can maintain its identity only if at least some identifiable matter remains in it all the time; otherwise it is no more the same body than the wine in a cask that is continuously emptied and refilled is the same wine. But just this is the fallacy: it does not follow, if difference in a certain respect at a certain time suffices to show non-identity, that sameness in that respect over a period of time is necessary to identity. Thus, Sir John Cutler's famous pair of stockings were the same pair all the time, although they started as silk and by much mending ended as worsted; people have found it hard to see this, because if at a given time there is a silk pair and also a worsted pair then there are two pairs. Again, it is clear that the same man may be in Birmingham at noon and in Oxford at 7 p.m., even though a man in Birmingham and a man in Oxford at a given time must be two different men. Once formulated, the fallacy is obvious, but it might be deceptive if not formulated.

'Why worry even about material continuity? Would not mental continuity be both necessary and sufficient?' Necessary, but not sufficient. Imagine a new 'Tichborne' trial. The claimant knows all the things he ought to know, and talks convincingly to the long-lost heir's friends. But medical evidence about scars and old fractures and so on indicates that he cannot be the man; moreover, the long-lost heir's corpse is decisively identified at an exhumation. Such a case would bewilder us, particularly if the claimant's *bona fides* were manifest. (He might, for example, voluntarily take a lie-detecting test.) But we should certainly not allow the evidence of mental connexions with the long-lost heir to settle the matter in the claimant's favour: the claimant cannot be the long-lost heir, whose body we know lies buried in Australia, and if he honestly thinks he is then we must try to cure him of a delusion.

'But if I went on being conscious, why should I worry which body I have?' To use the repeated 'I' prejudges the issue; a fairer way of putting the point would be: If there is going to be a consciousness that includes ostensible memories of my life, why should I worry about which body this consciousness goes with? When we put it that way, it is quite easy to imagine circumstances in which one would worry—particularly if the ostensible memories of my life were to be produced by processes that can produce entirely spurious memories.

If, however, memory is not enough for personal identity; if a man's living again does involve some bodily as well as mental continuity with the man who lived formerly; then we might fairly call his new bodily life a resurrection. So the upshot of our whole argument is that unless a man comes to life again by resurrection, he does not live again after death. At best some mental remnant of him would survive death; and I should hold that the possibility even of such survival involves at least a permanent *capacity* for renewed human life; if reincarnation is excluded, this means: a capacity for resurrection. It may be hard to believe in the resurrection of the body: but Aquinas argued in his commentary on I Corinthians 15, which I have already cited, that it is much harder to believe in an immortal but permanently disembodied human soul; for that would mean believing that a soul, whose very identity depends on the capacity for reunion with one human body rather than an-other, will continue to exist forever with this capacity unrealized.

Speaking of the resurrection, St. Paul used the simile of a seed that is planted and grows into an ear of corn, to show the relation between the corpse and the body that rises again from the dead. This simile fits in well enough with our discussion. In this life, the bodily aspect of person-al identity requires a one-one relationship and material continuity; one baby body grows into one old man's body by a continuous process. Now similarly there is a one-one re-lationship between the buried seed and the ear that grows out of it; one seed grows into one ear, one ear comes from one seed; and the ear of corn is materially continuous with the seed but need not have any material identity with it.

There is of course no philosophical reason to expect that from a human corpse there will arise at some future date a new human body, continuous in some way with the corpse; and in some particular cases there appear strong empirical objections. But apart from the *possibility* of resurrection, it seems to me a mere illusion to have any hope for life after death. I am of the mind of Judas

Maccabeus: if there is no resurrection, it is superfluous and vain to pray for the dead.

The traditional faith of Christianity, inherited from Judaism, is that at the end of this age Messiah will come and men will rise from their graves to die no more. That faith is not going to be shaken by inquiries about bodies burned to ashes or eaten by beasts; those who might well suffer just such death in martyrdom were those who were most confident of a glorious reward in the resurrection. One who shares that hope will hardly wish to take out an occultistic or philosophical insurance policy, to guarantee some sort of survival as an annuity, in case God's promise of resurrection should fail.

SURVIVAL AND THE IDEA OF "ANOTHER WORLD"

H. H. Price

As you all know, this year is the seventieth anniversary of the foundation of the Society for Psychical Research. From the very beginning, the problem of Survival has been one of the main interests of the Society; and that is my excuse, if any excuse is needed, for discussing some aspects of the problem this evening. I shall not, however, talk about the evidence for Survival. In this lecture I am only concerned with the conception of Survival; with the *meaning* of the Survival Hypothesis, and not with its truth or falsity. When we consider the Survival Hypothesis, whether we believe it or disbelieve it, what is it that we have in mind? Can we form any idea, even a rough and

H. H. Price was formerly Wykeham Professor of Logic in the University of Oxford. His writings include *Perception* (1932), *Hume's Theory of the External World* (1940), *Thinking and Experience* (1953), and *Belief* (1969). He has twice been President of the Society for Psychical Research. This lecture was delivered at a General Meeting of the Society on July 16, 1952, and was printed in the Society's *Proceedings*, Volume 50, Part 182, January 1953. It is reprinted here with the permission of the author and the Society.

provisional one, of what a disembodied human life might be like? Supposing we cannot, it will follow that what is called the Survival Hypothesis is a mere set of words and not a hypothesis at all. The evidence adduced in favour of it might still be evidence for something, and perhaps for something important, but we should no longer have the right to claim that it is evidence for Survival. There cannot be evidence for something which is completely unintelligible to us.

Now let us consider the situation in which we find ourselves after seventy years of psychical research. A very great deal of work has been done on the problem of Survival, and much of the best work by members of our Society. Yet there are the widest differences of opinion about the results. A number of intelligent persons would maintain that we now have a very large mass of evidence in favour of Survival; that some of it is of very good quality indeed, and cannot be explained away unless we suppose that the supernormal cognitive powers of some embodied human minds are vastly more extensive and more accurate than we can easily believe them to be; in short, that on the evidence available the Survival Hypothesis is more probable than not. Some people—and not all of them are silly or credulous—would even maintain that the Survival Hypothesis is proved, or as near to being so as any empirical hypothesis can be. On the other hand, there are also many intelligent persons who entirely reject these conclusions. Some of them, no doubt, have not taken the trouble to examine the evidence. But others of them have; they may even have given years of study to it. They would agree that the evidence is evidence of *something*, and very likely of something important. But, they would say, it cannot be evidence of Survival; there *must* be some alternative explanation of it, however difficult it may be to find out. Why do they take this line? I think it is because they find the very conception of Survival unintelligible. The very idea of a 'discarnate human personality' seems to them a muddled or absurd one; indeed not an idea at all, but just a phrase—an emotionally exciting one, no doubt—to which no clear meaning can be given.

Moreover, we cannot just ignore the people who have not examined the evidence. Some of our most intelligent and most highly educated contemporaries are among them. These men are well aware, by this time, that the evidence does exist, even if their predecessors fifty years ago were not. If you asked them why they do not trouble to examine it in detail, they would be able to offer reasons for their attitude. And one of their reasons, and not the least

weighty in their eyes, is the contention I mentioned just
now, that the very idea of Survival is a muddled or absurd
one. To borrow an example from Whately Carington, we know
pretty well what we mean by asking whether Jones has survived a shipwreck. We are asking whether he continues to
live after the shipwreck has occurred. Similarly it makes
sense to ask whether he survived a railway accident, or the
bombing of London. But if we substitute 'his own death'
for 'a shipwreck,' and ask whether he has survived it, our
question (it will be urged) becomes unintelligible. Indeed,
it *looks* self-contradictory, as if we were asking whether
Jones is still alive at a time when he is no longer alive
—whether Jones is both alive and not alive at the same
time. We may try to escape from this logical absurdity by
using phrases like 'discarnate existence', 'alive, but disembodied'. But such phrases, it will be said, have no
clear meaning. No amount of facts, however well established, can have the slightest tendency to support a meaningless hypothesis, or to answer an unintelligible question.
It would therefore be a waste of time to examine such facts
in detail. There are other and more important things to do.

If I am right so far, questions about the meaning of
the word 'survival' or of the phrase 'life after death' are
not quite so arid and academic as they may appear. Anyone
who wants to maintain that there is empirical evidence for
Survival ought to consider these questions, whether he
thinks the evidence strong or weak. Indeed, anyone who
thinks there is a *problem* of Survival at all should ask
himself what his conception of Survival is.

Now why should it be thought that the very idea of
life after death is unintelligible? Surely it is easy
enough to conceive (whether or not it is true) that experiences might occur after Jones's death which are linked with
experiences which he had before his death, in such a way
that his personal identity is preserved? But, it will be
said, the idea of after-death *experiences* is just the difficulty. What kind of experiences could they conceivably be?
In a disembodied state, the supply of sensory stimuli is
perforce cut off, because the supposed experient has no
sense organs and no nervous system. There can therefore be
no sense-perception. One has no means of being aware of
material objects any longer; and if one has not, it is hard
to see how one could have any emotions or wishes either.
For all the emotions and wishes we have in this present
life are concerned directly or indirectly with material objects, including of course our own organisms and other organisms, especially other human ones. In short, one could

only be said to have experiences at all, if one is aware of some sort of a *world*. In this way, the idea of Survival is bound up with the idea of 'another world' or a 'next world'. Anyone who maintains that the idea of Survival is after all intelligible must also be claiming that we can form some conception, however rough and provisional, of what 'the next world' or 'the other world' might be like. The sceptics I have in mind would say that we can form no such conception at all; and this, I think, is one of the main reasons why they hold that the conception of Survival itself is unintelligible. I wish to suggest, on the contrary, that we *can* form some conception, in outline at any rate, of what a 'next world' or 'another world' might be like, and consequently of the kind of experiences which disembodied minds, if indeed there are such, might be supposed to have.

The thoughts which I wish to put before you on this subject are not at all original. Something very like them is to be found in the chapter on Survival in Whately Carington's book *Telepathy*, and in the concluding chapter of Professor C. J. Ducasse's book *Nature, Mind and Death*.[1] Moreover, if I am not mistaken, the Hindu conception of *Kama Loka* (literally 'the world of desire') is essentially the same as the one which I wish to discuss; and something very similar is to be found in Mahayana Buddhism. In these two religions, of course, there is not just one 'other world' but several different 'other worlds', which we are supposed to experience in succession; not merely the Next World, but the next but one, and another after that. But I think it will be quite enough for us to consider just the Next World, without troubling ourselves about any additional Other Worlds which there might be. It is a sufficiently difficult task, for us Western people, to convince ourselves that it makes sense to speak of any sort of after-death world at all. Accordingly, with your permission, I shall use the expressions 'next world' and 'other world' interchangeably. If anyone thinks this an over-simplification, it will be easy for him to make the necessary corrections.

The Next World, I think, might be conceived as a kind of dream-world. When we are asleep, sensory stimuli are cut off, or at any rate are prevented from having their normal effects upon our brain-centres. But we still manage to have experiences. It is true that sense-perception no longer occurs, but something sufficiently like it does. In

---

[1] C. J. Ducasse, *Nature, Mind and Death* (La Salle, Illinois, Open Court Publishing Co., 1951).

sleep, our image-producing powers, which are more or less
inhibited in waking life by a continuous bombardment of
sensory stimuli, are released from this inhibition. And
then we are provided with a multitude of objects of awareness, about which we employ our thoughts and towards which
we have desires and emotions. Those objects which we are
aware of behave in a way which seems very queer to us when
we wake up. The laws of their behaviour are not the laws
of physics. But however queer their behaviour is, it does
not at all disconcert us at the time, and our personal
identity is not broken.

In other words, my suggestion is that the Next World,
if there is one, might be a world of mental images. Nor
need such a world be so 'thin and unsubstantial' as you
might think. Paradoxical as it may sound, there is nothing
imaginary about a mental image. It is an actual entity, as
real as anything can be. The seeming paradox arises from
the ambiguity of the verb 'to imagine'. It does sometimes
mean 'to have mental images'. But more usually it means
'to entertain propositions without believing them'; and
very often they are false propositions, and moreover we
*dis*believe them in the act of entertaining them. This is
what happens, for example, when we read Shakespeare's play
The Tempest, and that is why we say that Prospero and Ariel
are 'imaginary characters'. Mental images are not in this
sense imaginary at all. We do actually experience them,
and they are no more imaginary than sensations. To avoid
the paradox, though at the cost of some pedantry, it would
be well to distinguish between *imagining* and *imaging*, and
to have two different adjectives 'imaginary' and 'imagy'.
In this terminology, it is imaging, and not imagining, that
I wish to talk about; and the Next World, as I am trying to
conceive of it, is an *imagy* world, but not on that account
an imaginary one.

Indeed, to those who experienced it an image-world
would be just as 'real' as this present world is; and perhaps so like it, that they would have considerable difficulty in realising that they were dead. We are, of course,
sometimes told in mediumistic communications that quite a
lot of people do find it difficult to realise that they are
dead; and this is just what we should expect if the Next
World is an image-world. Lord Russell and other philosophers have maintained that a material object in this present
physical world is nothing more nor less than a complicated
system of *appearances*. So far as I can see, there might be
a set of visual images related to each other perspectively,
with front views and side views and back views all fitting
neatly together in the way that ordinary visual appearances

do now. Such a group of images might contain tactual
images too. Similarly it might contain auditory images
and smell images. Such a family of inter-related images
would make a pretty good object. It would be quite a
satisfactory substitute for the material objects which we
perceive in this present life. And a whole world composed
of such families of mental images would make a perfectly
good world.

It is possible, however, and indeed likely, that some
of those images would be what Francis Galton called *generic*
images. An image representing a dog or a tree need not
necessarily be an exact replica of some individual dog or
tree one has perceived. It might rather be a representation
of a *typical* dog or tree. Our memories are more specific
on some subjects than on others. How specific they are,
depends probably on the degree of interest we had in the
individual objects or events at the time when we perceived
them. An event which moved us deeply is likely to be re-
membered specifically and in detail; and so is an individual object to which we were much attached (for example, the
home of our childhood). But with other objects which interested us less and were less attended to, we retain only
a 'general impression' of a whole class of objects collec-
tively. Left to our own resources, as we should be in the
Other World, with nothing but our memories to depend on, we
should probably be able to form only generic images of such
objects. In this respect, an image-world would not be an
exact replica of this one, not even of those parts of this
one which we have actually perceived. To some extent it
would be, so to speak, a generalised picture, rather than a
detailed reproduction.

Let us now put our question in another way, and ask
what kind of experience a disembodied human mind might be
supposed to have. We can then answer that it might be an
experience in which *imaging* replaces sense-perception; 'replaces' it, in the sense that imaging would perform much
the same function as sense-perception performs now, by providing us with objects about which we could have thoughts,
emotions and wishes. There is no reason why we should not
be 'as much alive', or at any rate *feel* as much alive, in
an image-world as we do now in this present material world,
which we perceive by means of our sense-organs and nervous
systems. And so the use of the word 'survival' ('life
after death') would be perfectly justifiable.

It will be objected, perhaps, that one cannot be said
to be alive unless one has a body. But what is meant here
by 'alive'? It is surely conceivable (whether or not it is

true) that *experiences* should occur which are not causally connected with a physical organism. If they did, should we or should we not say that 'life' was occurring? I do not think it matters much whether we answer Yes or No. It is purely a question of definition. If you define 'life' in terms of certain very complicated physico-chemical processes, as some people would, then of course life after death is by definition impossible, because there is no longer anything to be alive. In that case, the problem of survival (*life* after bodily death) is misnamed. Instead, it ought to be called the problem of after-death *experiences*. And this is in fact the problem with which all investigators of the subject have been concerned. After all, what people want to know, when they ask whether we survive death, is simply whether experiences occur after death, or what likelihood, if any, there is that they do; and whether such experiences, if they do occur, are linked with each other and with *ante mortem* ones in such a way that personal identity is preserved. It is not physico-chemical processes which interest us, when we ask such questions. But there is another sense of the words 'life' and 'alive' which may be called the psychological sense; and in this sense 'being alive' just *means* 'having experiences of certain sorts'. In this psychological sense of the word 'life', it is perfectly intelligible to ask whether there is life after death, even though life in the physiological sense does *ex hypothesi* come to an end when someone dies. Or, if you like, the question is whether one could *feel* alive after bodily death, even though (by hypothesis) one would not *be* alive at that time. It will be just enough to satisfy most of us if the *feeling* of being alive continues after death. It will not make a halfpennyworth of difference that one will not then *be* alive in the physiological or biochemical sense of the word.

It may be said, however, that 'feeling alive' (life in the psychological sense) cannot just be equated with having experiences in general. Feeling alive, surely, consists in having experiences of a special sort, namely *organic sensations*—bodily feelings of various sorts. In our present experience, these bodily feelings are not as a rule separately attended to unless they are unusually intense or unusually painful. They are a kind of undifferentiated mass in the background of consciousness. All the same, it would be said, they constitute our feeling of being alive; and if they were absent (as surely they must be when the body is dead) the feeling of being alive could not be there.

I am not at all sure that this argument is as strong as it looks. I think we should still feel alive—or alive

enough—provided we experienced emotions and wishes, even
if no organic sensations accompanied these experiences, as
they do now. But in case I am wrong here, I would suggest
that *images* of organic sensations could perfectly well provide what is needed. We can quite well image to ourselves
what it feels like to be in a warm bath, even when we are
not actually in one; and a person who has been crippled can
image what it felt like to climb a mountain. Moreover, I
would ask whether we do not feel alive when we are dreaming.
It seems to me that we obviously do—or at any rate quite
alive enough to go on.

      This is not all. In an image-world, a dream-like
world such as I am trying to describe, there is no reason
at all why there should not be *visual* images resembling the
body which one had in this present world. In this present
life (for all who are not blind) visual percepts of one's
own body form as it were the constant centre of one's perceptual world. It is perfectly possible that visual images
of one's own body might perform the same function in the
next. They might form the continuing centre or nucleus of
one's image world, remaining more or less constant while
other images altered. If this were so, we should have an
additional reason for expecting that recently dead people
would find it difficult to realise that they were dead,
that is, disembodied. To all appearances they *would* have
bodies just as they had before, and pretty much the same
ones. But, of course, they might discover in time that
these image-bodies were subject to rather peculiar causal
laws. For example, it might be found that in an image-
world our wishes tend *ipso facto* to fulfil themselves in a
way they do not now. A wish to go to Oxford might be immediately followed by the occurrence of a vivid and detailed
set of Oxford-like images; even though, at the moment before, one's images had resembled Piccadilly Circus or the
palace of the Dalai Lama in Tibet. In that case, one would
realise that 'going somewhere'—transferring one's body
from one place to another—was a rather different process
from what it had been in the physical world. Reflecting on
such experiences, one might come to the conclusion that
one's body was not after all the same as the physical body
one had before death. One might conclude perhaps that it
must be a 'spiritual' or 'psychical' body, closely resembling the old body in appearance, but possessed of rather
different causal properties. It has been said, of course,
that phrases like 'spiritual body' or 'psychical body' are
utterly unintelligible, and that no conceivable empirical
meaning could be given to such expressions. But I would
suggest that they might be a way (rather a misleading way

perhaps) of referring to a set of body-like images. If our
supposed dead empiricist continued his investigations, he
might discover that his whole world—not only his own body,
but everything else he was aware of—had different causal
properties from the physical world, even though everything
in it had shape, size, colour and other qualities which material objects have now. And so eventually, by the exercise of ordinary inductive good sense, he could draw the
conclusion that he was in 'the next world' or 'the other
world' and no longer in this one. If, however, he were a
very dogmatic philosopher, who distrusted inductive good
sense and preferred *a priori* reasoning, I do not know what
condition he would be in. Probably he would never discover
that he was dead at all. Being persuaded, on *a priori*
grounds, that life after death was impossible, he might in-
sist on thinking that he must still be in this world, and
refuse to pay any attention to the new and strange causal
laws which more empirical thinkers would notice.

I think, then, that there is no difficulty in conceiving that the experience of feeling alive could occur in the
absence of a physical organism; or, if you prefer to put it
so, a disembodied personality could *be* alive in the psychological sense, even though by definition it would not be
alive in the physiological or biochemical sense.

Moreover, I do not see why disembodiment need involve
the destruction of personal identity. It is, of course,
sometimes supposed that personal identity depends on the
continuance of a background of organic sensation—the 'mass
of bodily feeling' mentioned before. (This may be called
the Somato-centric Analysis of personal identity.) We must
notice, however, that this background of organic sensation
is not literally the same from one period of time to another. The very most that can happen is that the organic sensations which form the background of my experience now
should be *exactly similar* to those which were the background of my experience a minute ago. And as a matter of
fact the present ones need not *all* be exactly similar to
the previous ones. I might have a twinge of toothache now
which I did not have then. I may even have an overall feeling of lassitude now which I did not have a minute ago, so
that the whole mass of bodily feeling, and not merely one
part of it, is rather different; and this would not inter-
rupt my personal identity at all. The most that is required is only that the majority (not all) of my organic
sensations should be closely (not exactly) similar to those
I previously had. And even this is only needed if the two
occasions are close together in my private time series; the
organic sensations I have now might well be very unlike

those I used to have when I was one year old. I say 'in my
private time series'. For when I wake up after eight hours
of dreamless sleep my personal identity is not broken,
though in the physical or public time series there has been
a long interval between the last organic sensations I experienced before falling asleep, and the first ones I experience when I wake up. But if similarity, and not literal
sameness, is all that is required of this 'continuing organic background', it seems to me that the continuity of it
could be perfectly well preserved if there were organic *images* after death very like the organic *sensations* which occurred before death.

   As a matter of fact, this whole 'somato-centric' analysis of personal identity appears to me highly disputable.
I should have thought that Locke was much nearer the truth
when he said that personal identity depends on memory. But
I have tried to show that even if the 'somato-centric' theory of personal identity is right, there is no reason why
personal identity need be broken by bodily death, provided
there are images after death which sufficiently resemble
the organic sensations one had before; and this is very
like what happens when one falls asleep and begins dreaming.

   There is, however, another argument against the con-
ceivability of a disembodied person, to which some present-
day Linguistic Philosophers would attach great weight. It
is neatly expressed by Mr. A.G.N. Flew when he says, 'People are what you meet.'[2] By 'a person' we are supposed to
mean a human organism which behaves in certain ways, and
especially one which speaks and can be spoken to. And when
we say, 'This is the same person whom I saw yesterday', we
are supposed to mean just that it is the same human organism which I saw yesterday, and also that it behaves in a
recognisably similar way.

   'People are what you meet.' With all respect to Mr.
Flew, I would suggest that he does not in this sense 'meet'
himself. He might indeed have had one of those curious out-
of-body experiences which are occasionally mentioned in our

---

[2]*University*, Vol. ii, no. 2, p. 38; in a symposium on
'Death' with Professor D. M. Mackinnon. Mr. Flew obviously
uses 'people' as the plural of 'person'; but if we are to
be linguistic, I am inclined to think that the *nuances* of
'people' are not quite the same as those of 'person'. When
we use the word 'person', in the singular or the plural,
the notion of consciousness is more prominently before our
minds than it is when we use the word 'people'.

records, and he might have seen his own body from outside
(if he has, I heartily congratulate him); but I do not
think we should call this 'meeting'. And surely the important question is, what constitutes my personal identity *for
myself*. It certainly does not consist in the fact that
other people can 'meet' me. It might be that I was for myself the same person as before, even at a time when it was
quite impossible for others to meet me. No one can 'meet'
me when I am dreaming. They can, of course, come and look
at my body lying in bed; but this is not 'meeting', because
no sort of social relations are then possible between them
and me. Yet, although temporarily 'unmeetable', during my
dreams I am still, for myself, the same person that I was.
And if I went on dreaming *in perpetuum*, and could never be
'met' again, this need not prevent me from continuing to be,
for myself, the same person.

　　As a matter of fact, however, we can quite easily conceive that 'meeting' of a kind might still be possible between discarnate experients. And therefore, even if we do
make it part of the definition of 'a person', that he is
capable of being met by others, it will still make sense to
speak of 'discarnate persons', provided we allow that telepathy is possible between them. It is true that a special
sort of telepathy would be needed; the sort which in this
life produces *telepathic apparitions*. It would not be sufficient that A's thoughts or emotions should be telepathically affected by B's. If such telepathy were sufficiently
prolonged and continuous, and especially if it were recip-
rocal, it would indeed have some of the characteristics of
social intercourse; but I do not think we should call it
'meeting', at any rate in Mr. Flew's sense of the word. It
would be necessary, in addition, that A should be aware of
something which could be called 'B's body', or should have
an experience not too unlike the experience of *seeing* another person in this life. This additional condition would be
satisfied if A experienced a telepathic apparition of B.
It would be necessary, further, that the telepathic apparition by means of which B 'announces himself' (if one may
put it so) should be recognisably similar on different occasions. And if it were a case of meeting some person
again whom one had previously known in this world, the telepathic apparition would have to be recognisably similar to
the physical body which that person had when he was still
alive.

　　There is no reason why an image-world should not contain a number of images which are telepathic apparitions;
and if it did, one could quite intelligently speak of 'meeting other persons' in such a world. All the experiences I

have when I meet another person in this present life could still occur, with only this difference, that percepts would be replaced by images. It would also be possible for another person to 'meet' me in the same manner, if I, as telepathic agent, could cause him to experience a suitable telepathic apparition, sufficiently resembling the body I used to have when he formerly 'met' me in this life.

I now turn to another problem which may have troubled some of you. If there be a next world, *where* is it? Surely it must be somewhere. But there does not seem to be any room for it. We can hardly suppose that it is up in the sky (i.e. outside the Earth's atmosphere) or under the surface of the earth, as Homer and Vergil seemed to think. Such suggestions may have contented our ancestors, and the Ptolemaic astronomy may have made them acceptable, for some ages, even to the learned; but they will hardly content us. Surely the next world, if it exists, must be somewhere; and yet, it seems, there is nowhere for it to be.

The answer to this difficulty is easy if we conceive of the Next World in the way I have suggested, as a dreamlike world of mental images. Mental images, including dream images, are in a space of their own. They do have spatial properties. Visual images, for instance, have extension and shape, and they have spatial relations to one another. But they have no spatial relation to objects in the physical world. If I dream of a tiger, my tiger-image has extension and shape. The dark stripes have spatial relations to the yellow parts, and to each other; the nose has a spatial relation to the tail. Again, the tiger image as a whole may have spatial relations to another image in my dream, for example to an image resembling a palm tree. But suppose we have to ask how far it is from the foot of my bed, whether it is three inches long, or longer, or shorter; is it not obvious that these questions are absurd ones? We cannot answer them, not because we lack the necessary information or find it impracticable to make the necessary measurements, but because the questions themselves have no meaning. In the space of the physical world these images are nowhere at all. But in relation to other images of mine, each of them is somewhere. Each of them is extended, and its parts are in spatial relations to one another. There is no *a priori* reason why all extended entities must be in physical space.

If we now apply these considerations to the Next World, as I am conceiving of it, we see that the question 'where is it?' simply does not arise. An image-world would have a space of its own. We could not find it anywhere in the space of the physical world, but this would not in the least prevent it from being a spatial world all the same. If you like, it would be its own 'where'.[3]

I am tempted to illustrate this point by referring to the fairytale of Jack and the Beanstalk. I am not of course suggesting that we should take the story seriously. But if we were asked to try to make sense of it, how should we set about it? Obviously the queer world which Jack found was not at the top of the beanstalk in the literal, spatial sense of the words 'at the top of'. Perhaps he found some very large pole rather like a beanstalk, and climbed up it. But (we shall say) when he got to the top he suffered an abrupt change of consciousness, and began to have a dream or waking vision of a strange country with a giant in it. To choose another and more respectable illustration: In Book VI of Vergil's *Aeneid*, we are told how Aeneas descended into the Cave of Avernus with the Sibyl and walked from there into the Other World. If we wished to make the narrative of the illustrious poet intelligible, how should we set about it? We should suppose that Aeneas did go down into the cave, but that once he was there he suffered a change of consciousness, and all the strange experiences which happened afterwards—seeing the River Styx, the Elysian Fields and the rest—were part of a dream or vision which he had. The space he passed through in his journey was an image-space, and the River Styx was not three Roman miles, or any other number of miles, from the cave in which his body was.

It follows that when we speak of 'passing' from this world to the next, this passage is not to be thought of as any sort of movement in space. It should rather be thought of as a change of consciousness, analogous to the change which occurs when we 'pass' from waking experience to dreaming. It would be a change from the perceptual type of conciousness to another type of consciousness in which perception ceases and imaging replaces it, but unlike the change from waking consciousness to dreaming in being irreversible. I suppose that nearly everyone nowadays who talks of 'passing' from this world to the other does think of the transition in this way, as some kind of irreversible change of consciousness, and not as a literal spatial transition in which one goes from one place to another place.

---

[3]Conceivably its geometrical structure might also be different from the geometrical structure of the physical world. In that case the space of the Next World would not only be other than the space of the physical world, but would also be a different *sort* of space.

So much for the question 'where the next world is', if
there be one. I have tried to show that if the next world
is conceived as a world of mental images, the question simply does not arise. I now turn to another difficulty. It
may be felt that an image-world is somehow a deception and
a sham, not a *real* world at all. I have said that it would
be a kind of dream-world. Now when one has a dream in this
life, surely the things one is aware of in the dream are
not *real* things. No doubt the dreamer really does have
various mental images. These images do actually occur.
But this is not all that happens. As a result of having
these images, the dreamer believes, or takes for granted,
that various material objects exist and various physical
events occur; and these beliefs are mistaken. For example,
he believes that there is a wall in front of him and that
by a mere effort of will he succeeds in flying over the top
of it. But the wall did not really exist, and he did not
really fly over the top of it. He was in a state of delusion. Because of the images which he did really have,
there *seemed* to him to be various objects and events which
did not really exist at all. Similarly, you may argue, it
may *seem* to discarnate minds (if indeed there are such)
that there is a world in which they live, and a world not
unlike this one. If they have mental images of the appropriate sort, it may even *seem* to them that they have bodies
not unlike the ones they had in this life. But surely they
will be mistaken? It is all very well to say, with the
poet, that 'dreams are real while they last'—that dream-
objects are only called 'unreal' when one wakes up, and
normal sense perceptions begin to occur with which the
dream experiences can be contrasted. And it is all very
well to conclude from this that if one did *not* wake up, if
the change from sense-perception to imaging were irreversible, one would not call one's dream objects unreal, because
there would then be nothing with which to contrast them.
But would they not still *be* unreal for all that? Surely
discarnate minds, according to my account of them, would be
in a state of permanent delusion; whereas a dreamer in this
life (fortunately for him) is only in a temporary one. And
the fact that a delusion goes on for a long time, even for
ever and ever, does not make it any the less delusive. De-
lusions do not turn themselves into realities just by going
on and on. Nor are they turned into realities by the fact
that their victim is deprived of the power of detecting
their delusiveness.

Now, of course, if it were true that the next life
(supposing there is one) is a condition of permanent delusion, we should just have to put up with it. We might not

like it; we might think that a state of permanent delusion
is a bad state to be in. But our likes and dislikes are
irrelevant to the question. I would suggest, however, that
this argument about the 'delusiveness' or 'unreality' of an
image-world is based on a confusion.

One may doubt whether there is any clear meaning in
using the words 'real' and 'unreal' *tout court*, in this perfectly general and unspecified way. One may properly say,
'this is real silver, and that is not', 'this is a real
pearl and that is not', or again 'this is a real pool of
water, and that is only a mirage'. The point here is that
something X is mistakenly believed to be something else Y,
because it does resemble Y in some respects. It makes perfectly good sense, then, to say that X is not really Y.
This piece of plated brass is not real silver, true enough.
It only looks like silver. But for all that, it cannot be
called 'unreal' in the unqualified sense, in the sense of
not existing at all. Even the mirage is something, though
it is not the pool of water you took it to be. It is a
perfectly good set of visual appearances, though it is not
related to other appearances in the way you thought it was;
for example, it does not have the relations to tactual appearances, or to visual appearances from other places,
which you expected it to have. You may properly say that
the mirage is not a real pool of water, or even that it is
not a real physical object, and that anyone who thinks it
is must be in a state of delusion. But there is no clear
meaning in saying that it is just 'unreal' *tout court*, without any further specification or explanation. In short,
when the word 'unreal' is applied to something, one means
that it is different from something else, with which it
might be mistakenly identified; what that something else is
may not be explicitly stated, but it can be gathered from
the context.

What, then, could people mean by saying that a next
world such as I have described would be 'unreal'? If they
are saying anything intelligible, they must mean that it is
different from something else, something else which it does
resemble in some respects, and might therefore be confused
with. And what is that something else? It is this present
physical world in which we now live. An image-world, then,
is only 'unreal' in the sense that it is not really physical, though it might be mistakenly thought to be physical
by some of those who experience it. But this only amounts
to saying that the world I am describing would be an *other*
world, other than this present physical world, which is
just what it ought to be; other than this present physical
world, and yet sufficiently like it to be possibly confused

with it, because images do resemble percepts. And what
would this otherness consist in? First, in the fact that
it is in a *space* which is other than physical space; secondly, and still more important, in the fact that the
causal laws of an image-world would be different from the
laws of physics. And this is also our ground for saying
that the events we experience in dreams are 'unreal', that
is, not really physical, though mistakenly believed by the
dreamer to be so. They do in some ways closely resemble
physical events, and that is why the mistake is possible.
But the causal laws of their occurrence are quite different,
as we recognise when we wake up; and just occasionally we
recognise it even while we are still asleep.
    Now let us consider the argument that the inhabitants
of the Other World, as I have described it, would be in a
state of delusion. I admit that some of them might be.
That would be the condition of the people described in the
mediumistic communications already referred to—the people
who 'do not realise that they are dead'. Because their
images are so like the normal percepts they were accustomed
to in this life, they believe mistakenly that they are
still living in the physical world. But, as I have already
tried to explain, their state of delusion need not be permanent and irremediable. By attending to the relations between one image and another, and applying the ordinary inductive methods by which we ourselves have discovered the
causal laws of this present world in which *we* live, they
too could discover in time what the causal laws of *their*
world are. These laws, we may suppose, would be more like
the laws of Freudian psychology than the laws of physics.
And once the discovery was made, they would be cured of
their delusion. They would find out, perhaps with surprise,
that the world they were experiencing was *other* than the
physical world which they experienced before, even though
in some respects like it.

    Let us now try to explore the conception of a world of
mental images a little more fully. Would it not be a '*subjective*' world? And surely there would be many *different*
next worlds, not just one; and each of them would be private. Indeed, would there not be as many next worlds as
there are discarnate minds, and each of them wholly private
to the mind which experiences it? In short, it may seem
that each of us, when dead, would have his own dream world,
and there would be no common or public Next World at all.
    'Subjective', perhaps, is rather a slippery word. Cer-
tainly, an image world would have to be subjective in the
sense of being mind-dependent, dependent for its existence

upon mental processes of one sort or another; images, after all, are mental entities. But I do not think that such a world need be completely private, if telepathy occurs in the next life. I have already mentioned the part which telepathic apparitions might play in it, in connection with Mr. Flew's contention that 'people are what you meet'.[4] But there is more to be said. It is reasonable to suppose that in a disembodied state telepathy would occur more frequently than it does now. It seems likely that in this present life our telepathic powers are constantly being inhibited by our need to adjust ourselves to our physical environment. It even seems likely that many telepathic 'impressions' which we receive at the unconscious level are shut out from consciousness by a kind of biologically-motivated censorship. Once the pressure of biological needs is removed, we might expect that telepathy would occur continually, and manifest itself in consciousness by modifying and adding to the images which one experiences. (Even in this life, after all, some dreams are telepathic.)

If this is right, an image-world such as I am describing would not be the product of one single mind only, nor would it be purely private. It would be the joint-product of a group of telepathically-interacting minds and public to all of them. Nevertheless, one would not expect it to have unrestricted publicity. It is likely that there would still be *many* next worlds, a different one for each group of like-minded personalities. I admit I am not quite sure what might be meant by 'like-minded' and 'unlike-minded' in this connection. Perhaps we could say that two personalities are like-minded if their memories or their characters are sufficiently similar. It might be that Nero and Marcus Aurelius do not have a world in common, but Socrates and Marcus Aurelius do.

So far, we have a picture of many 'semi-public' next worlds, if one may put it so; each of them composed of mental images, and yet not wholly private for all that, but public to a limited group of telepathically-interacting minds. Or, if you like, after death everyone does have his own dream, but there is still some overlap between one person's dream and another's, because of telepathy.

I have said that such a world would be mind-dependent, even though dependent on a group of minds rather than a single mind. In what way would it be mind-dependent? Presumably in the same way as dreams are now. It would be dependent on the *memories* and the *desires* of the persons who

---

[4]Cf. pp. 30-31.

experienced it. Their memories and their desires would determine what sort of images they had. If I may put it so,
the 'stuff' or 'material' of such a world would come in the
end from one's memories, and the 'form' of it from one's desires. To use another analogy, memory would provide the
pigments, and desire would paint the picture. One might expect, I think, that desires which had been unsatisfied in
one's earthly life would play a specially important part in
the process. That may seem an agreeable prospect. But
there is another which is less agreeable. Desires which
had been *repressed* in one's earthly life, because it was
too painful or too disgraceful to admit that one had them,
might also play a part, and perhaps an important part, in
determining what images one would have in the next. And
the same might be true of repressed memories. It may be
suggested that what Freud (in one stage of his thought)
called 'the censor'—the force or barrier or mechanism
which keeps some of our desires and memories out of consciousness, or only lets them in when they disguise themselves in symbolic and distorted forms—operates only in
this present life and not in the next. However we conceive
of 'the censor', it does seem to be a device for enabling
us to adapt ourselves to our environment. And when we no
longer have an environment, one would expect that the barrier would come down.

    We can now see that an after-death world of mental
images can also be quite reasonably described in the terminology of the Hindu thinkers as 'a world of desire' (*Kama
Loka*). Indeed, this is just what we should expect if we
assume that dreams, in this present life, are the best
available clue to what the next life might be like. Such
a world could also be described as 'a world of memories';
because imaging, in the end, is a function of memory, one
of the ways in which our memory-dispositions manifest themselves. But this description would be less apt, even
though correct as far as it goes. To use the same rather
inadequate language as before, the 'materials' out of which
an image-world is composed would have to come from the memories of the mind or group of minds whose world it is. But
it would be their desires (including those repressed in
earthly life) which determined the ways in which these memories were used, the precise kind of dream which was built
up out of them or on the basis of them.

    It will, of course, be objected that memories cannot
exist in the absence of a physical brain, nor yet desires,
nor images either. But this proposition, however plausible,
is after all just an empirical hypothesis, not a necessary
truth. Certainly there is empirical evidence in favour of

it. But there is also empirical evidence against it.
Broadly speaking one might say, perhaps, that the 'normal'
evidence tends to support this Materialistic or Epiphenomenalist theory of memories, images and desires, whereas the
'supernormal' evidence on the whole tends to weaken the
Materialist or Epiphenomenalist theory of human personality
(of which this hypothesis about the brain-dependent character of memories, images and desires is a part). Moreover,
any evidence which directly supports the Survival Hypothesis
(and there is quite a lot of evidence which does, provided
we are prepared to admit that the Survival Hypothesis is
intelligible at all) is *pro tanto* evidence against the Materialistic conception of human personality.

In this lecture, I am not of course trying to argue in
favour of the Survival Hypothesis. I am only concerned
with the more modest task of trying to make it intelligible.
All I want to maintain, then, is that there is nothing self-
contradictory or logically absurd in the hypothesis that
memories, desires and images can exist in the absence of a
physical brain. The hypothesis may, of course, be false.
My point is only that it is not absurd; or, if you like,
that it is at any rate intelligible, whether true or not.
To put the question in another way, when we are trying to
work out for ourselves what sort of thing a discarnate life
might conceivably be (if there is one) we have to ask what
kind of *equipment*, so to speak, a discarnate mind might be
supposed to have. It cannot have the power of sense-perception, nor the power of acting on the physical world by
means of efferent nerves, muscles and limbs. What would it
have left? What could we take out with us, as it were,
when we pass from this life to the next? What we take out
with us, I suggest, can only be our memories and desires,
and the power of constructing out of them an image world to
suit us. Obviously we cannot take our material possessions
out with us; but I do not think this is any great loss, for
if we remember them well enough and are sufficiently attached to them, we shall be able to construct image-replicas
of them which will be just as good, and perhaps better.

In this connection I should like to mention a point
which has been made several times before. Both Whately Carington and Professor Ducasse have referred to it, and no
doubt other writers have. But I believe it is of some importance and worth repeating. Ecclesiastically-minded critics sometimes speak rather scathingly of the 'materialistic'
character of mediumistic communications. They are not at
all edified by these descriptions of agreeable houses, beautiful landscapes, gardens and the rest. And then, of course,
there is Raymond Lodge's notorious cigar. These critics

complain that the Next World as described in these communications is no more than a reproduction of this one, slightly improved perhaps. And the argument apparently is that
the 'materialistic' character of the communications is evidence against their genuineness. On the contrary, as far
as it goes, it is evidence *for* their genuineness. Most people in this life do like material objects and are deeply interested in them. This may be deplorable, but there it is.
If so, the image-world they would create for themselves in
the next life might be expected to have just the 'materialistic' character of which these critics complain. If one
had been fond of nice houses and pleasant gardens in this
life, the image-world one would create for oneself in the
next might be expected to contain image-replicas of such objects, and one would make these replicas as like 'the real
thing' as one's memories permitted; with the help, perhaps,
of telepathic influences from other minds whose tastes were
similar. This would be all the more likely to happen if
one had not been able to enjoy such things in this present
life as much as one could wish.

But possibly I have misunderstood the objection which
these ecclesiastical critics are making. Perhaps they are
saying that if the Next World is like this, life after
death is not worth having. Well and good. If they would
prefer a different sort of Next World, and find the one
described in these communications insipid or unsatisfying
to their aspirations, then they can expect to get a different one—in fact, just the sort of next world they want.
They have overlooked a crucial point which seems almost
obvious; that if there is an after-death life at all, there
must surely be many next worlds, separate from and as it
were impenetrable to one another, corresponding to the *different* desires which different groups of discarnate personalities have. [5]

The belief in life after death is often dismissed as
'mere wish-fulfilment'. Now it will be noticed that the
Next World as I have been trying to conceive of it is precisely a wish-fulfilment world, in much the same sense in
which some dreams are described as wish-fulfilments.
Should not this make a rational man very suspicious of the
ideas I am putting before you? Surely this account of the
Other World is 'too good to be true'? I think not. Here
we must distinguish two different questions. The question
whether human personality continues to exist after death is

[5]Cf p. 37.

a question of fact, and wishes have nothing to do with it
one way or the other. But *if* the answer to this factual
question were 'Yes' (and I emphasise the 'if'), wishes
might have a very great deal to do with the kind of world
which discarnate beings would live in. Perhaps it may be
helpful to consider a parallel case. It is a question of
fact whether dreams occur in this present life. It has to
be settled by empirical investigation, and the wishes of
the investigators have nothing to do with it. It is just a
question of what the empirical facts are, whether one likes
them or not. Nevertheless, granting that dreams do occur,
a man's wishes might well have a very great deal to do with
determining what the content of his dreams is to be; especially unconscious wishes on the one hand, and on the other,
conscious wishes which are not satisfied in waking life.
Of course the parallel is not exact. There is one very important difference between the two cases. With dreams, the
question of fact is settled. It is quite certain that many
people do have dreams. But in the case of Survival, the
question of fact is not settled, or not at present. It is
still true, however, that though wishes have nothing to do
with it, they might have a very great deal to do with the
kind of world we should live in after death, *if* we survive
death at all.

But perhaps this does not altogether dispose of the
objection that my account of the Other World is 'too good
to be true'. Surely a sober-minded and cautious person
would be very shy of believing that there is, or even could
be, a world in which all our wishes are fulfilled? How
very suspicious we are about travellers' tales of Eldorado
or descriptions of idyllic South Sea islands! Certainly we
are, and on good empirical grounds. For they are tales
about this present material world; and we know that matter
is very often recalcitrant to human wishes. But in a dream-
world Desire is king. This objection would only hold good
if the world I am describing were supposed to be some part
of the *material* world—another planet perhaps, or the Earthly Paradise of which some poets have written. But the Next
World as I am trying to conceive of it (or rather Next
Worlds, for we have seen that there would be many different
ones) is not of course supposed to be a part of the material world at all. It is a dream-like world of mental images.
True enough, some of these images might be expected to resemble some of the material objects with which we are familiar now; but only if, and to the extent that, their percip-
ients *wanted* this resemblance to exist. There is every
reason, then, for being suspicious about descriptions of
this present material world, or alleged parts of it, on the

ground that they are 'too good to be true'; but when it is
a 'country of the mind' (if one may say so) which is being
described, these suspicions are groundless. A purely mind-
dependent world, if such a world there be, would *have* to be
a wish-fulfilment world.

Nevertheless, likes and dislikes, however irrelevant
they may be, do of course have a powerful psychological influence upon us when we consider the problem of Survival;
not only when we consider the factual evidence for or
against, but also when we are merely considering the theoretical implications of the Survival Hypothesis itself, as
I am doing now. It is therefore worth while to point out
that the Next World as I am conceiving of it need not necessarily be an agreeable place at all. If arguments about
what is good or what is bad did have any relevance, a case
could be made out for saying that this conception of the
Next World is 'too bad to be true', rather than too good.
As we have seen, we should have to reckon with many different Next Worlds, not just with one. The world you would
experience after death would depend upon the kind of person
you are. And if what I have said so far has any sense in
it, we can easily conceive that some people's Next Worlds
would be much more like purgatories than paradises—and
pretty unpleasant purgatories too.

This is because there are *conflicting* desires within
the same person. Few people, if any, are completely inte-
grated personalities, though some people come nearer to it
than others. And sometimes when a man's desires appear
(even to himself) to be more or less harmonious with one
another, the appearance is deceptive. His conscious desires do not conflict with one another, or not much; but
this harmony has only been achieved at the cost of repression. He has unconscious desires which conflict with the
neatly organised pattern of his conscious life. If I was
right in suggesting that repression is a biological phenomenon, if the 'threshold' between conscious and unconscious
no longer operates in a disembodied state, or operates much
less effectively, this seeming harmony will vanish after
the man is dead. To use scriptural language, the secrets
of his heart will be revealed—at any rate to himself.
These formerly repressed desires will manifest themselves by
appropriate images, and these images might be exceedingly
horrifying—as some dream-images are in this present life,
and for the same reason. True enough, they will be 'wish-
fulfilment' images, like everything else that he experiences
in the Next World as I am conceiving it. But the wishes
they fulfil will conflict with other wishes which he also
has. And the emotional state which results might be worse

than the worst nightmare; worse, because the dreamer cannot
wake up from it. For example, in his after-death dream
world he finds himself doing appallingly cruel actions. He
never did them in his earthly life. Yet the desire to do
them was there, even though repressed and unacknowledged.
And now the lid is off, and this cruel desire fulfils itself by creating appropriate images. But unfortunately for
his comfort, he has benevolent desires as well, perhaps
quite strong ones; and so he is distressed and even horrified by these images, even though there is also a sense in
which they are just the ones he wanted. Of course his benevolent desires too may be expected to manifest themselves
by appropriate wish-fulfilment images. But because there
is this conflict in his nature, they will not wholly satisfy him either. There will be something in him which rejects them as tedious and insipid. It is a question of the
point of view, if one cares to put it so. Suppose a person
has two conflicting desires A and B. Then from the point
of view of desire A, the images which fulfil desire B will
be unsatisfying, or unpleasant, or even horrifying; and
vice versa from the point of view of desire B. And unfortunately, both points of view belong to the same person.
He occupies both of them at once.

This is not all. If psycho-analysts are right, there
is such a thing as a desire to be punished. Most people,
we are told, have guilt-feelings which are more or less
repressed; we have desires, unacknowledged or only half-
acknowledged, to suffer for the wrongs we have done. These
desires too will have their way in the Next World, if my
picture of it is right, and will manifest themselves by
images which fulfil them. It is not a very pleasant prospect, and I need not elaborate it. But it looks as if
everyone would experience an image-purgatory which exactly
suits him. It is true that his unpleasant experiences
would not literally be punishments, any more than terrify-
ing dreams are in this present life. They would not be inflicted upon him by any external judge; though, of course,
if we are Theists, we shall hold that the laws of nature,
in other worlds as in this one, are in the end dependent on
the will of a Divine Creator. Each man's purgatory would
be just the automatic consequence of his own desires; if
you like, he would punish himself by having just those images which his own good-feelings demand. But, if there is
any consolation in it, he would have these unpleasant experiences because he *wanted* to have them; exceedingly unpleasant as they might be, there would still be something
in him which was satisfied by them.

There is another aspect of the conflict of desires. Every adult person has what we call 'a character'; a set of more or less settled and permanent desires, with the corresponding emotional dispositions, expressing themselves in a more or less predictable pattern of thoughts, feelings, and actions. But it is perfectly possible to desire that one's character should be different, perhaps very different, from what it is at present. This is what philosophers call a 'second-order' desire, a desire that some of one's own desires should be altered. Such second-order desires are not necessarily ineffective, as New Year resolutions are supposed to be. People can within limits alter their own characters, and sometimes do; and if they succeed in doing so, it is in the end because they *want* to. But these 'second-order' desires—desires to alter one's own character— are seldom effective immediately; and even when they appear to be, as in some cases of religious conversion, there has probably been a long period of subconscious or unconscious preparation first. To be effective, desires of this sort must occur again and again. I must go on wishing to be more generous or less timid, and not just wish it on New Year's day; I must train myself to act habitually—and think too—in the way that I should act and think if I possessed the altered character for which I wish. From the point of view of the present moment, however, one's character is something fixed and given. The wish I have at half-past twelve to-day will do nothing, or almost nothing, to alter it.

These remarks may seem very remote from the topic I am supposed to be discussing. But they have a direct bearing on a question which has been mentioned before[6]: whether, or in what sense, the Next World as I am conceiving of it should be called a 'subjective' world. As I have said already, a Next World such as I have described *would* be subjective, in the sense of mind-dependent. The minds which experience it would also have created it. It would just be the manifestation of their own memories and desires, even though it might be the joint creation of a number of telepathically interacting minds, and therefore not wholly private. But there is a sense in which it might have a certain objectivity all the same. One thing we mean by calling something 'objective' is that it is so whether we like it or not, and even if we dislike it. This is also what we mean by talking about 'hard facts' or 'stubborn facts'.

---

[6]Cf. p. 36.

At first sight it may seem that in an image-world such as I have described there could be no hard facts or stubborn facts, and nothing objective in this sense of the word 'objective'. How could there be, if the world we experience is itself a wish-fulfilment world? But a man's character *is* in this sense 'objective'; objective in the sense that he has it whether he likes it or not. And facts about his character are as 'hard' or 'stubborn' as any. Whether I like it or not, and even though I dislike it, it is a hard fact about me that I am timid or spiteful, that I am fond of eating oysters or averse from talking French. I may wish sometimes that these habitual desires and aversions of mine were different, but at any particular moment this wish will do little or nothing to alter them. In the short run, a man's permanent and habitual desires are something 'given', which he must accept and put up with as best he can, even though in the very long run they are alterable.

Now in the next life, according to my picture of it, it would be these permanent and habitual desires which would determine the nature of the world in which a person has to live. His world would be, so to speak, the outgrowth of his character; it would be his own character represented to him in the form of dream-like images. There is therefore a sense in which he gets exactly the sort of world he wants, whatever internal conflicts there may be between one of these wants and another. Yet he may very well dislike having the sort of character he does have. In the short run, as I have said, his character is something fixed and given, and objective in the sense that he has that character whether he likes it or not. Accordingly his image-world is also objective in the same sense. It is objective in the sense that it insists on presenting itself to him whether he likes it or not.

To look at the same point in another way: the Next World as I am picturing it may be a very queer sort of world, but still it would be subject to causal laws. The laws would not, of course, be the laws of physics. As I have suggested already, they might be expected to be more like the laws of Freudian psychology. But they would be laws all the same, and objective in the sense that they hold good whether one liked it or not. And if we do dislike the image-world which our desires and memories create for us—if, when we get what we want, we are horrified to discover what things they were which we wanted—we shall have to set about altering our characters, which might be a very long and painful process.

Some people tell us, of course, that all desires, even the most permanent and habitual ones, will wear themselves

out in time by the mere process of being satisfied. It may
be so, and perhaps there is some comfort in the thought.
In that case the dream-like image world of which I have
been speaking would only be temporary, and we should have
to ask whether after the Next World there is a next one.
The problem of Survival would then arise again in a new
form. We should have to ask whether personal identity
could still be preserved when we were no longer even dreaming. It could, I think, be preserved through the transition from this present perceptible world to a dream-like
image world of the kind I have been describing. But if
even imaging were to cease, would there be anything left of
human personality at all? Or would the state of existence
—if any—which followed be one to which the notion of personality, at any rate our present notion, no longer had any
application? I think that these are questions upon which
it is unprofitable and perhaps impossible to speculate.
(If anyone wishes to make the attempt, I can only advise
him to consult the writings of the mystics, both Western
and Oriental.) It is quite enough for us to consider what
the *next* world might conceivably be like, and some of you
may think that even this is too much.

   Before I end, I should like to make one concluding
remark. You may have noticed that the Next World, according to my account of it, is not at all unlike what some
metaphysicians say *this* world is. In the philosophy of
Schopenhauer, this present world itself, in which we now
live, is a world of 'will and idea'. And so it is in
Berkeley's philosophy too; material objects are just collections of 'ideas', though according to Berkeley the will
which presents these ideas to us is the will of God, acting
directly upon us in a way which is in effect telepathic.
Could it be that these Idealist metaphysicians have given
us a substantially correct picture of the next world,
though a mistaken picture of this one? The study of metaphysical theories is out of fashion nowadays. But perhaps
students of psychical research would do well to pay some
attention to them. *If* there are other worlds than this
(again I emphasise the 'if') who knows whether with some
stratum of our personalities we are not living in them now,
as well as in this present one which conscious sense-perception discloses? Such a repressed and unconscious awareness
of a world different from this one might be expected to
break through into consciousness occasionally in the course
of human history, very likely in a distorted form, and this
might be the source of those very queer ideas which we read
of with so much incredulity and astonishment in the writings of some speculative metaphysicians. Not knowing their

source, they mistakenly applied these ideas to this world in which we now live, embellishing them sometimes with an elaborate facade of deductive reasoning. Viewed in cold blood and with a sceptical eye, their attempts may appear extremely unconvincing, and their deductive reasoning fallacious. But perhaps, without knowing it, they may have valuable hints to give us if we are trying to form some conception, however tentative, of 'another world'. And this is something we must try to do if we take the problem of Survival seriously.

Part Two The Resurrection of the Body

THE RESURRECTION OF CHRIST AND THE RESURRECTION OF MEN

St. Paul

Now if Christ be preached that he rose from the dead, how say some among you that there is no resurrection of the dead? But if there be no resurrection of the dead, then is Christ not risen: and if Christ be not risen, then is our preaching vain, and your faith is also vain. Yea, and we found false witnesses of God; because we have testified of God that he raised up Christ: whom he raised not up, if so be that the dead rise not. For if the dead rise not, then is not Christ raised: and if Christ be not raised, your faith is vain; ye are yet in your sins. Then they also which are fallen asleep in Christ are perished. If in this life only we have hope in Christ, we are of all men most miserable. But now is Christ risen from the dead, and become the first fruits of them that slept. For since by man came death, by man came also the resurrection of the dead. For as in Adam all die, so in Christ shall all be made alive. . . .
But some man will say, How are the dead raised up? and with what body do they come? Thou fool, that which thou sowest is not quickened, except it die: and that which thou sowest, thou sowest not that body that shall be, but bare grain, it may chance of wheat, or of some other grain: but God giveth it a body as it hath pleased him, and to every seed his own body. All flesh is not the same flesh: but there is one kind of flesh of men, another flesh of beasts, another of fishes, and another of birds. There are also celestial bodies, and bodies terrestrial: but the glory of the celestial is one, and the glory of the terrestrial is another. There is one glory of the sun, and another glory of the moon, and another glory of the stars; for one star differeth from another star in glory. So also is the resurrection of the dead. It is sown in corruption, it is raised in incorruption: it is sown in dishonour, it is raised in glory: it is sown in weakness, it is raised in

The First Epistle to the Corinthians, Chapter 15, verses 12-22 and 35-57; The King James Version.

power: it is sown a natural body, it is raised a spiritual
body. There is a natural body, and there is a spiritual
body. And so it is written, The first man Adam was made
a living soul; the last Adam was made a quickening spirit.
Howbeit that was not first which is spiritual, but that
which is natural; and afterward that which is spiritual.
The first man is of the earth, earthy; the second man is
the Lord from heaven. As is the earthy, such are they also
that are earthy: and as is the heavenly, such are they also
that are heavenly. And as we have borne the image of the
earthy, we shall also bear the image of the heavenly.

Now this I say, brethren, that flesh and blood cannot
inherit the kingdom of God; neither doth corruption inherit
incorruption. Behold, I show you a mystery; we shall not
all sleep, but we shall all be changed, in a moment, in the
twinkling of an eye, at the last trump: for the trumpet
shall sound, and the dead shall be raised incorruptible,
and we shall be changed. For this corruptible must put on
incorruption, and this mortal must put on immortality. So
when this corruptible shall have put on incorruption, and
this mortal shall have put on immortality, then shall be
brought to pass the saying that is written, Death is swallowed up in victory. O death, where is thy sting? O grave,
where is thy victory? The sting of death is sin; and the
strength of sin is the law. But thanks be to God, which
giveth us the victory through our Lord Jesus Christ.

IMMORTALITY OF THE SOUL OR RESURRECTION OF THE DEAD? THE WITNESS OF THE NEW TESTAMENT

Oscar Cullmann

PREFACE

The present work is the translation of a study already published in Switzerland,[1] of which a summary has appeared in various French periodicals.

No other publication of mine has provoked such enthusiasm or such violent hostility. The editors of the periodicals concerned have been good enough to send me some of the letters of protest which they have received from their readers. One of the letter-writers was prompted by my

Oscar Cullmann is Professor of the Theological Faculty of the University of Basel and of the Sorbonne in Paris, and a Member, *Institut de France*. He is one of the leading New Testament scholars of our day. His writings include *Christ and Time* (1945, English translation 1951), and *The Christology of the New Testament* (1957, English translation 1959).
The work printed here was delivered as the Ingersoll Lecture on the Immortality of Man at Harvard University in 1955 and was published in book form by the Epworth Press, London, in 1958. It is reprinted here with the author's permission. [Editor's note: The preface contains the author's response to criticisms of earlier versions of the views expressed in this lecture and might perhaps be read afterward by those new to them.

A brief comment is necessary concerning the untranslated term *Heilsgeschichte*. In the English version of Dr. Cullmann's *Christ and Time* this is translated as "redemptive history." Its use here reflects the author's insistence that the Christian proclamation must be understood not as a presentation of timeless truths to which actual occurrences are irrelevant but as the claim that salvation has been made available by specific historical events in time.]

[1]*Mélanges* offers à Karl Barth à l'occasion de ses 70 ans (publ. by Reinhardt, Bâle, 1956) (*Theologische Zeitschrift*, N. 2, pp. 126 ff). See also *Verbum Caro* (1956), pp. 58 ff.

article to reflect bitterly that 'the French people, dying
for lack of the Bread of Life, have been offered instead
of bread, stones, if not serpents'. Another writer takes
me for a kind of monster who delights in causing spiritual
distress. 'Has M. Cullmann', he writes, 'a stone instead
of a heart?' For a third, my study has been 'the cause of
astonishment, sorrow, and deep distress'. Friends who have
followed my previous work with interest and approval have
indicated to me the pain which this study has caused them.
In others I have detected a malaise which they have tried
to conceal by an eloquent silence.

My critics belong to the most varied camps. The contrast, which out of concern for the truth I have found it
necessary to draw between the courageous and joyful primitive Christian hope of the resurrection of the dead and the
serene philosophic expectation of the survival of the immortal soul, has displeased not only many sincere Christians in all Communions and of all theological outlooks,
but also those whose convictions, while not outwardly alien-
ated from Christianity, are more strongly moulded by philosophical considerations. So far, no critic of either kind
has attempted to refute me by exegesis, that being the
basis of our study.

This remarkable agreement seems to me to show how
widespread is the mistake of attributing to primitive
Christianity the Greek belief in the immortality of the
soul. Further, people with such different attitudes as
those I have mentioned are united in a common inability to
listen with complete objectivity to what the texts teach us
about the faith and hope of primitive Christianity, without
mixing their own opinions and the views that are so dear to
them with their interpretation of the texts. This inability to listen is equally surprising on the part of intelligent people committed to the principles of sound, scientific
exegesis and on the part of believers who profess to rely
on the revelation in Holy Scripture.

The attacks provoked by my work would impress me more
if they were based on exegetical arguments. Instead, I am
attacked with very general considerations of a philosophical, psychological, and above all sentimental kind. It has
been said against me, 'I can accept the immortality of the
soul, but not the resurrection of the body', or 'I cannot
believe that our loved ones merely sleep for an indeterminate period, and that I myself, when I die, shall merely
sleep while awaiting the resurrection'.

Is it really necessary today to remind intelligent
people, whether Christians or not, that there is a difference between recognizing that such a view was held by

Socrates and accepting it, between recognizing a hope as
primitive Christian and sharing it oneself?

We must first listen to what Plato and St Paul said.
We can go farther. We can respect and indeed admire both
views. How can we fail to do so when we see them in relation to the life and death of their authors? But that is
no reason for denying a radical difference between the
Christian expectation of the resurrection of the dead and
the Greek belief in the immortality of the soul. However
sincere our admiration for both views, it cannot allow us
to pretend, against our profound conviction and against the
exegetical evidence, that they are compatible. That it is
possible to discover certain points of contact, I have
shown in this study; but that does not prevent their fundamental inspiration being totally different.

The fact that later Christianity effected a link between the two beliefs and that today the ordinary Christian
simply confuses them has not persuaded me to be silent
about what I, in common with most exegetes, regard as true;
and all the more so, since the link established between the
expectation of the 'resurrection of the dead' and the belief in 'the immortality of the soul' is not in fact a link
at all but renunciation of one in favour of the other.
1 Corinthians 15 has been sacrificed for the *Phaedo*. No
good purpose is served by concealing this fact, as is often
done today when things that are really imcompatible are com-
bined by the following type of over-simplified reasoning:
that whatever in early Christian teaching appears to us irreconcilable with the immortality of the soul, viz. the
resurrection of the body, is not an *essential* affirmation
for the first Christians but simply an accommodation to the
mythological expressions of the thought of their time, and
that the heart of the matter is the immortality of the soul.
On the contrary we must recognize loyally that precisely
those things which distinguish the Christian teaching from
the Greek belief are at the heart of primitive Christianity.
Even if the interpreter cannot himself accept it as fundamental, he has no right to conclude that it was not fundamental for the authors whom he studies.

In view of the negative reactions and 'distress' provoked by the publication of my thesis in various periodicals, should I not have broken off the debate for the sake
of Christian charity, instead of publishing this booklet?
My decision has been determined by the conviction that
'stumbling-blocks' are sometimes salutary, both from the
scholarly and the Christian point of view. I simply ask my
readers to be good enough to take the trouble of reading on
till the end.

The question is here raised in its exegetical aspect.
If we turn to the Christian aspect, I would venture to remind my critics that when they put in the forefront, as
they do, the particular manner in which they *wish* themselves and their loved ones to survive, they are involun-
tarily giving grounds to the opponents of Christianity who
constantly repeat that the faith of Christians is nothing
more than the projection of their desires.

In reality, does it not belong to the greatness of our
Christian faith, as I have done my best to expound it, that
we do not begin from our personal desires but place our
resurrection within the framework of a cosmic redemption
and of a new creation of the universe?

I do not under-estimate in any way the difficulty one
may experience in sharing this faith, and I freely admit
the difficulty of talking about this subject in a dispas-
sionate manner. An open grave at once reminds us that we
are not simply concerned with a matter of academic discussion. But is there not therefore all the more reason for
seeking truth and clarity at this point? The best way to
do it is not by beginning with what is ambiguous, but by
explaining simply and as faithfully as possible, with all
the means at our disposal, the hope of the New Testament
authors, and thus showing the very essence of this hope and
—however hard it may seem to us—what it is that separates
it from other beliefs we hold so dear. If in the first
place we examine objectively the primitive Christian expectation in those aspects which seem shocking to our commonly
accepted views, are we not following the only possible way
by which it may perhaps none the less be given us, not only
to understand that expectation better, but also to ascer-
tain that it is not so impossible to accept it as we imagine.

I have the impression that some of my readers have not
troubled to read my exposition right through. The comparison of the death of Socrates with that of Jesus seems to
have scandalized and irritated them so much that they have
read no farther, and have not looked at what I have said
about the New Testament faith in the victory of Christ over
death.

For many of those who have attacked me the cause of
'sorrow and distress' has been not only the distinction we
draw between resurrection of the dead and immortality of
the soul, but above all the place which I with the whole of
primitive Christianity believe should be given to the intermediate state of those who are dead and die in Christ before the final days, the state which the first-century authors described by the word 'sleep'. The idea of a temporary
state of waiting is all the more repugnant to those who

would like fuller information about this 'sleep' of the
dead who, though stripped of their fleshly bodies, are
still deprived of their resurrection bodies although in
possession of the Holy Spirit. They are not able to observe the discretion of the New Testament authors, including St Paul, in this matter; or to be satisfied with the
joyful assurance of the Apostle when he says that hence-
forth death can no longer separate from Christ him who has
the Holy Spirit. 'Whether we live or die, we belong to
Christ.'

There are some who find this idea of 'sleep' entirely
unacceptable. I am tempted to lay aside for a moment the
exegetical methods of this study and ask them whether they
have never experienced a dream which has made them happier
than any other experience, even though they have only been
sleeping. Might that not be an illustration, though indeed
an imperfect one, of the state of anticipation in which,
according to St Paul, the dead in Christ find themselves
during their 'sleeping' as they wait for the resurrection
of the body?

However that may be, I do not intend to avoid the
'stumbling-block' by minimizing what I have said about the
provisional and still imperfect character of this state.
The fact is that, according to the first Christians the
full, genuine life of the resurrection is inconceivable
apart from the new body, the 'spiritual body', with which
the dead will be clothed when heaven and earth are re-
created.

In this study I have referred more than once to the
Isenheim altar-piece by the medieval painter Grünewald.
It was the resurrection body that he depicted, not the im-
mortal soul. Similarly, another artist, John Sebastian
Bach, has made it possible for us to hear, in the Credo of
the Mass in B Minor, the musical interpretation of the
words of this ancient creed which faithfully reproduces the
New Testament faith in Christ's resurrection and our own.
The jubilant music of this great composer is intended to
express not the immortality of the soul but the event of
the resurrection of the body: *Et resurrexit tertia die* . . .
Expecto resurrectionem mortuorum et vitam venturi saeculi.
And Handel, in the last part of the *Messiah*, gives us some
inkling of what St Paul understood by the sleep of those
who rest in Christ; and also, in the song of triumph,
Paul's expectation of the final resurrection when the 'last
trumpet shall sound and we shall be changed'.

Whether we share this hope or not, let us at least admit that in this case the artists have proved the best ex-
positors of the Bible.

INTRODUCTION

If we were to ask an ordinary Christian today (whether well-read Protestant or Catholic, or not) what he conceived to be the New Testament teaching concerning the fate of man after death, with few exceptions we should get the answer: 'The immortality of the soul.' Yet this widely-accepted idea is one of the greatest misunderstandings of Christianity. There is no point in attempting to hide this fact, or to veil it by reinterpreting the Christian faith. This is something that should be discussed quite candidly. The concept of death and resurrection is anchored in the Christ-event (as will be shown in the following pages), and hence is incompatible with the Greek belief in immortality; because it is based in *Heilsgeschichte* it is offensive to modern thought. Is it not such an integral element of the early Christian proclamation that it can neither be surrendered nor reinterpreted without robbing the New Testament of its substance?[2]

But is it really true that the early Christian resurrection faith is irreconcilable with the Greek concept of the immortality of the soul? Does not the New Testament, and above all the Gospel of John, teach that we already have eternal life? Is it really true that death in the New Testament is always conceived as 'the last enemy' in a way that is diametrically opposed to Greek thought, which sees in death a friend? Does not Paul write: 'O death, where is thy sting?' We shall see at the end that there *is* at least an analogy, but first we must stress the fundamental differences between the two points of view.

The widespread misunderstanding that the New Testament teaches the immortality of the soul was actually encouraged by the rock-like *post-Easter* conviction of the first disciples that the bodily Resurrection of Christ had robbed death of all its horror,[3] and that from the moment of

---

[2] See on the following also O. Cullmann, 'La foi à la résurrection et l'espérance de la résurrection dans le Nouveau Testament', *Etudes théol. et rel* (1943), pp. 3 ff; *Christ and Time* (1945), pp. 231 ff; Ph. H. Menoud, *Le sort des trépassés* (1945); R. Mehl, *Der letzte Feind* (1954).

[3] But hardly in such a way that the original Christian community could speak of 'natural' dying. This manner of speaking of Karl Barth's in *Die kirchliche Dogmatik*, III, 2 (1948), pp. 776 ff, though found in a section where otherwise the negative valuation of death as the 'last enemy' is

Easter onward, the Holy Spirit had awakened the souls of
believers into the life of the Resurrection.

The very fact that the words 'post-Easter' need to be
underlined illustrates the whole abyss which nevertheless
separates the early Christian view from that of the Greeks.
The whole of early Christian thought is based in *Heilsgeschichte*, and everything that is said about death and eternal life stands or falls with a belief in a real occurrence,
in real events which took place in time. This is the radical distinction from Greek thought. The purpose of my book
Christ and Time was precisely to show that this belongs to
the substance, to the essence of early Christian faith,
that it is something not to be surrendered, not to be altered in meaning; yet it has often been mistakenly thought
that I intended to write an essay on the New Testament attitude toward the problem of Time and Eternity.

If one recognizes that death and eternal life in the
New Testament are always bound up with the Christ-event,
then it becomes clear that for the first Christians the
soul is not intrinsically immortal, but rather became so
only through the resurrection of Jesus Christ, and through
faith in Him. It also becomes clear that death is not intrinsically the Friend, but rather that its 'sting', its
power, is taken away *only* through the victory of Jesus over
it in His death. And lastly, it becomes clear that the
resurrection already accomplished is not the state of fulfilment, for that remains in the future until the body is
also resurrected, which will not occur until 'the last day'.

It is a mistake to read into the Fourth Gospel an
early trend toward the Greek teaching of immortality, because there also eternal life is bound up with the Christ-
event. [4] Within the bounds of the Christ-event, of course,
the various New Testament books place the accent in different places, but common to all is the view of *Heilsgeschichte*. [5] Obviously one must reckon with Greek influence

---

[3] (cont.) strongly emphasized, still seems to me not to be
grounded in the New Testament. See 1 Corinthians 11:30 (on
that verse see below, pp. 74, 75).

[4] In so far as John's Gospel is rooted in *Heilsgeschichte*,
it is not true, as Rudolph Bultmann wrongly maintains, that
a process of demythologizing is already to be discerned in
it.

[5] As Bo Reicke correctly maintains, 'Einheitlichkeit oder
verschiedene Lehrbegriffe in der neutestamentlichen Theolo-
gie', *Theol. Zeitschr.*, 9 (1953), pp. 401 ff.

upon the origin of Christianity from the very beginning,[6] but so long as the Greek ideas are subordinated to the total view of *Heilsgeschichte*, there can be no talk of 'Hellenization' in the proper sense.[7] Genuine Hellenization occurs for the first time at a later date.

I THE LAST ENEMY: DEATH

Socrates and Jesus

Nothing shows more clearly than the contrast between the death of Socrates and that of Jesus (a contrast which was often cited, though for other purposes, by early opponents of Christianity) that the biblical view of death from the first is focused in salvation-history and so departs completely from the Greek conception.[8]

In Plato's impressive description of the death of Socrates, in the *Phaedo*, occurs perhaps the highest and most sublime doctrine ever presented on the immortality of the soul. What gives his argument its unexcelled value is his scientific reserve, his disclaimer of any proof having mathematical validity. We know the arguments he offers for the immortality of the soul. Our body is only an outer garment which, as long as we live, prevents our soul from moving freely and from living in conformity to its proper eternal essence. It imposes upon the soul a law which is not appropriate to it. The soul, confined within the body, belongs to the eternal world. As long as we live, our soul finds itself in a prison, that is, in a body essentially alien to

---

[6]All the more as the Qumrân texts show that the Judaism to which embryonic Christianity was so closely connected was already itself influenced by Hellenism. See O. Cullmann, 'The Significance of the Qumrân Texts for Research into the Beginnings of Christianity', *Journ. of Bibl. Lit.*, 74 (1955), pp. 213 ff. See, too, Rudolf Bultmann, *Theology of the New Testament* (1955), Vol. II, p. 13 note.

[7]Rather, it would be more accurate to speak of a Christian 'historicization' (in the sense of *Heilsgeschichte*) of the Greek ideas. Only in this sense, not in that employed by Bultmann, are the New Testament 'myths' already 'demythologized' by the New Testament itself.

[8]Material on this contrast in E. Benz, *Der gekreuzigte Gerechte bei Plato im N. T. und in der alten Kirche* (1950).

it. Death, in fact, is the great liberator. It looses the chains, since it leads the soul out of the prison of the body and back to its eternal home. Since body and soul are radically different from one another and belong to different worlds, the destruction of the body cannot mean the destruction of the soul, any more than a musical composition can be destroyed when the instrument is destroyed. Although the proofs of the immortality of the soul do not have for Socrates himself the same value as the proofs of a mathematical theorem, they nevertheless attain within their own sphere the highest possible degree of validity, and make immortality so probable that it amounts to a 'fair chance' for man. And when the great Socrates traced the arguments for immortality in his address to his disciples on the day of his death, he did not merely *teach* this doctrine: at that moment he lived his doctrine. He showed how we serve the freedom of the soul, even in this present life, when we occupy ourselves with the eternal truths of philosophy. For through philosophy we penetrate into that eternal world of ideas to which the soul belongs, and we free the soul from the prison of the body. Death does no more than complete this liberation. Plato shows us how Socrates goes to his death in complete peace and composure. The death of Socrates is a beautiful death. Nothing is seen here of death's terror. Socrates cannot fear death, since indeed it sets us free from the body. Whoever fears death proves that he loves the world of the body, that he is thoroughly entangled in the world of sense. Death is the soul's great friend. So he teaches; and so, in wonderful harmony with his teaching, he dies—this man who embodied the Greek world in its noblest form.

And now let us hear how Jesus dies. In Gethsemane He knows that death stands before Him, just as Socrates expected death on his last day. The Synoptic Evangelists furnish us, by and large, with a unanimous report. Jesus begins 'to tremble and be distressed', writes Mark (14:33). 'My soul is troubled, even to death', He says to His disciples.[9] Jesus is so thoroughly human that He shares the

---

[9]Despite the parallel Jonah 4:9 which is cited by E. Klostermann, *Das Markus-Evangelium*, 3rd Edition (1936), ad loc., and E. Lohmeyer, *Das Evangelium des Markus* (1937), ad loc., I agree with J. Weiss, *Das Markus-Evangelium*, 3rd Edition (1917), ad loc., that the explanation: 'I am so sad that I prefer to die' in this situation where Jesus *knows* that He is going to die (the scene is the Last Supper!) is completely unsatisfactory; moreover, Weiss's interpretation: 'My

natural fear of death.[10]   Jesus is afraid, though not as a
coward would be of the men who will kill Him, still less of
the pain and grief which precede death. He is afraid in
the face of death itself. Death for Him is not something
divine: it is something dreadful. Jesus does not want to
be alone in this moment. He knows, of course, that the
Father stands by to help Him. He looks to Him in this decisive moment as He has done throughout his life. He turns
to Him with all His human fear of this great enemy, death.
He is afraid of death. It is useless to try to explain
away Jesus' fear as reported by the Evangelists. The opponents of Christianity who already in the first centuries
made the contrast between the death of Socrates and the
death of Jesus saw more clearly here than the exponents of
Christianity. He was really afraid. Here is nothing of
the composure of Socrates, who met death peacefully as a
friend. To be sure, Jesus already knows the task which has
been given Him: to suffer death; and He has already spoken
the words: 'I have a baptism with which I must be baptized,
and *how distressed* (or *afraid*) *I am* until it is accomplished' (Luke 19:50). Now, when God's enemy stands before
Him, He cries to God, whose omnipotence He knows: 'All
things are possible with thee; let this cup pass from me'
(Mark 14:36). And when He concludes, 'Yet not as I will,
but as thou wilt', this does not mean that at the last He,
like Socrates, regards death as the friend, the liberator.

---

[9](cont.) affliction is so great that I am sinking under the
weight of it' is supported by Mark 15:34. Also Luke 12:50,
'How distressed I am until the baptism (= death) takes
place', allows of no other explanation.

[10]Old and recent commentators (J. Wellhausen, *Das Evangelium
Marci*, 2nd Edition (1909), ad. loc., J. Schniewind in *N. T.
Deutsch* (1934), ad loc., E. Lohmeyer, *Das Evangelium des
Markus* (1937), ad loc., seek in vain to avoid this conclusion, which is supported by the strong Greek expressions
for 'tremble and shrink', by giving explanations which do
not fit the situation, in which Jesus already knows that He
must suffer for the sins of His people (Last Supper). In
Luke 12:50 it is completely impossible to explain away the
'distress' in the face of death, and also in view of the
fact that Jesus is abandoned by God on the Cross (Mark
15:34), it is not possible to explain the Gethsemane scene
except through this distress at the prospect of being abandoned by God, an abandonment which will be the work of Death,
God's great enemy.

No, He means only this: If this greatest of all terrors,
death, must befall Me according to Thy will, then I submit
to this horror. Jesus knows that in itself, because death
is the enemy of God, to die means to be utterly forsaken.
Therefore He cries to God; in face of this enemy of God He
does not want to be alone. He wants to remain as closely
tied to God as He has been throughout His whole earthly
life. For whoever is in the hands of death is no longer in
the hands of God, but in the hands of God's enemy. At this
moment, Jesus seeks the assistance, not only of God, but
even of His disciples. Again and again He interrupts His
prayer and goes to His most intimate disciples, who are trying to fight off sleep in order to be awake when the men
come to arrest their Master. They try; but they do not succeed, and Jesus must wake them again and again. Why does
He want them to keep awake? He does not want to be alone.
When the terrible enemy, death, approaches, He does not
want to be forsaken even by the disciples whose human weakness He knows. 'Could you not watch one hour?' (Mark
14:37).

Can there be a greater contrast than that between Socrates and Jesus? Like Jesus, Socrates has his disciples
about him on the day of his death; but he discourses se-
renely with them on immortality. Jesus, a few hours before
His death, trembles and begs His disciples not to leave Him
alone. The author of the Epistle to the Hebrews, who, more
than any other New Testament author, emphasizes the full
deity (1:10) but also the full humanity of Jesus, goes
still farther than the reports of the three Synoptists in
his description of Jesus' fear of death. In 5:7 he writes
that Jesus 'with loud cries and tears offered up prayers
and supplications to Him who was able to save Him'.[11] Thus,
according to the Epistle to the Hebrews, Jesus wept and
cried in the face of death. There is Socrates, calmly and
composedly speaking of the immortality of the soul; here
Jesus, weeping and crying.

And then the death-scene itself. With sublime calm
Socrates drinks the hemlock; but Jesus (thus says the Evan-
gelist, Mark 15:34—we dare not gloss it over) cries: 'My
God, my God, why hast thou forsaken me?' And with another
inarticulate cry He dies (Mark 15:37). This is not 'death
as a friend'. This is death in all its frightful horror.
This is really '*the last enemy*' of God. This is the name

---

[11]The reference to Gethsemane here seems to me unmistakable.
J. Héring, *L'Epître aux Hébreaux* (1954), ad loc., concurs
in this.

Paul gives it in 1 Corinthians 15:26, where the whole contrast between Greek thought and Christianity is disclosed.[12] Using different words, the author of the Johannine Apocalypse also regards death as the last enemy, when he describes how at the end death will be cast into the lake of fire (20:14). Because it is God's enemy, it separates us from God, who is Life and the Creator of all life. Jesus, who is so closely tied to God, tied as no other man has even been, for precisely this reason must experience death much more terribly than any other man. To be in the hands of the great enemy of God means to be forsaken by God. In a way quite different from others, Jesus must suffer this abandonment, this separation from God, the only condition really to be feared. Therefore He cries to God: 'Why hast thou forsaken me?' He is now actually in the hands of God's great enemy.

We must be grateful to the Evangelists for having glossed over nothing at this point. Later (as early as the beginning of the second century, and probably even earlier) there were people who took offence at this—people of Greek provenance. In early Christian history we call them Gnostics.

I have put the death of Socrates and the death of Jesus side by side. For nothing shows better the radical difference between the Greek doctrine of the immortality of the soul and the Christian doctrine of the Resurrection. Because Jesus underwent death in all its horror, not only in His body, but also in His soul ('My God, why hast thou forsaken me'), and as He is regarded by the first Christians as the Mediator of salvation, He must indeed be the very one who in His death conquers death itself. He cannot obtain this victory by simply living on as an immortal soul, thus fundamentally *not* dying. He can conquer death only by actually dying, by betaking Himself to the sphere of death, the destroyer of life, to the sphere of 'nothingness', of abandonment by God. When one wishes to overcome someone else, one must enter his territory. Whoever wants to conquer death must die; he must really cease to live—not

---

[12]The problem is presented in entirely false perspective by J. Leipoldt, *Der Tod bei Griechen und Juden* (1942). To be sure, he correctly makes a sharp distinction between the Greek view of death and the Jewish. But Leipoldt's efforts always to equate the Christian with the Greek and oppose it to the Jewish only become comprehensible when one notes the year in which this book was published and the series (*Germanentum, Christentum und Judentum*) of which it is a part.

simply live on as an immortal soul, but die in body and soul, lose life itself, the most precious good which God has given us. For this reason the Evangelists, who none the less intended to present Jesus as the Son of God, have not tried to soften the terribleness of His thoroughly human death.

Furthermore, if life is to issue out of so genuine a death as this, a new divine act of creation is necessary. And this act of creation calls back to life not just a part of the man, but the whole man—all that God had created and death had annihilated. For Socrates and Plato no new act of creation is necessary. For the body is indeed bad and should not live on. And that part which is to live on, the soul, does not die at all.

If we want to understand the Christian faith in the Resurrection, we must completely disregard the Greek thought that the material, the bodily, the corporeal is bad and *must* be destroyed, so that the death of the body would not be in any sense a destruction of the true life. For Christian (and Jewish) thinking the death of the body is *also* destruction of God-created life. No distinction is made: even the life of our body is true life; death is the destruction of *all* life created by God. Therefore it is death and not the body which must be conquered by the Resurrection.

Only he who apprehends with the first Christians the horror of death, who takes death seriously as death, can comprehend the Easter exultation of the primitive Christian community and understand that the whole thinking of the New Testament is governed by belief in the Resurrection. Belief in the immortality of the soul is not belief in a revolutionary event. Immortality, in fact, is only a *negative* assertion: the soul does *not* die, but simply lives on. Resurrection is a *positive* assertion: the whole man, who has really died, is recalled to life by a new act of creation by God. Something has happened—a miracle of creation! For something has also happened previously, something fearful: life formed by God has been destroyed.

Death in itself is not beautiful, not even the death of Jesus. Death before Easter is really the Death's head surrounded by the odour of decay. And the death of Jesus is as loathsome as the great painter Grünewald depicted it in the Middle Ages. But precisely for this reason the same painter understood how to paint, along with it, in an incomparable way, the great victory, the Resurrection of Christ: Christ in the new body, the Resurrection body. Whoever paints a pretty death can paint no resurrection. Whoever has not grasped the horror of death cannot join Paul

in the hymn of victory: 'Death is swallowed up—in victory!
O death, where is thy victory?   O death, where is thy sting?'
(1 Corinthians 15:34 f).

II   THE WAGES OF SIN: DEATH

Body and Soul—Flesh and Spirit

Yet the contrast between the Greek idea of the immortality of the soul and the Christian belief in the resurrection is still deeper.   The belief in the resurrection
presupposes the Jewish connexion between death and *sin*.
Death is not something natural, willed by God, as in the
thought of the Greek philosophers; it is rather something
unnatural, abnormal, opposed to God.[13]   The Genesis narrative teaches us that it came into the world only by the sin
of man.   Death is a curse, and the whole creation has become involved in the curse.   The sin of man has necessita-
ted the whole series of events which the Bible records and
which we call the story of redemption.   Death can be conquered only to the extent that sin is removed.   For 'death
is the wages of sin'.   It is not only the Genesis narrative
which speaks thus.   Paul says the same thing (Romans 6:23),
and this is the view of death held by the whole of primitive Christianity.   Just as sin is something opposed to God,
so is its consequence, death.   To be sure, God can make use
of death (1 Corinthians 15:35 ff, John 12:24), as He can
make use of Satan to man.
     Nevertheless, death *as such* is the enemy of God.   For
God is Life and the Creator of life.   It is not by the will
of God that there are withering and decay, dying and sickness, the by-products of death working in our life.   All
these things, according to Christian and Jewish thinking,
come from human sin.   Therefore, every healing which Jesus
accomplishes is not only a driving back of death, but also
an invasion of the province of sin; and therefore on every
occasion Jesus says: 'Your sins are forgiven.'   Not as
though there were a corresponding sin for every individual

---

[13]We shall see that Death, in view of its conquest by
Christ, has lost all its horror.   But I still would not venture as does Karl Barth, *Die Kirchliche Dogmatik*, III, 2
(1948), p. 777 ff (on the basis of the 'second death' distinguished in Apocalypse 21:8), to speak in the name of the
New Testament of a 'natural death' (see 1 Corinthians 11:30!).

sickness; but rather, like the presence of death, the fact that sickness exists at all is a consequence of the sinful condition of the whole of humanity. Every healing is a partial resurrection, a partial victory of life over death. That is the Christian point of view. According to the Greek interpretation, on the contrary, bodily sickness is a corollary of the fact that the body is bad in itself and is ordained to destruction. For the Christian an anticipation of the Resurrection can already become visible, even in the earthly body.

That reminds us that the body is in no sense bad in itself, but is, like the soul, a gift of our Creator. Therefore, according to Paul, we have duties with regard to our body. God is the *Creator* of all things. The Greek doctrine of immortality and the Christian hope in the resurrection differ so radically because Greek thought has such an entirely different interpretation of creation. The Jewish and Christian interpretation of creation excludes the whole Greek dualism of body and soul. For indeed the visible, the corporeal, is just as truly God's creation as the invisible. God is the maker of the body. The body is not the soul's prison, but rather a temple, as Paul says (1 Corinthians 6:19): the temple of the Holy Spirit! The basic distinction lies here. Body and soul are not opposites. God finds the corporeal 'good' after He has created it. The Genesis story makes this emphasis explicit. Conversely, moreover, sin also embraces the whole man, not only the body, but the soul as well; and its consequence, death, extends over all the rest of creation. Death is accordingly something dreadful, because the whole visible creation, including our body, is something wonderful, even if it is corrupted by sin and death. Behind the pessimistic interpretation of death stands the optimistic view of creation. Wherever, as in Platonism, death is thought of in terms of liberation, there the visible world is not recognized directly as God's creation.

Now, it must be granted that in Greek thought there is also a very positive appreciation of the body. But in Plato the good and beautiful in the corporeal are not good and beautiful in virtue of corporeality but rather, so to speak, *in spite of* corporeality: the soul, the eternal and the only substantial reality of being, shines faintly through the material. The corporeal is not the real, the eternal, the divine. It is merely that through which the real appears—and then only in debased form. The corporeal is meant to lead us to contemplate the pure archetype, freed from all corporeality, the invisible Idea.

To be sure, the Jewish and Christian points of view also see something else besides corporeality. For the whole creation is corrupted by sin and death. The creation which we see is not as God willed it, as He created it; nor is the body which we wear. Death rules over all; and it is not necessary for annihilation to accomplish its work of destruction before this fact becomes apparent—it is already obvious in the whole outward form of all things. Everything, even the most beautiful, is marked by death. Thus it might seem as if the distinction between Greek and Christian interpretation is not so great after all. And yet it remains radical. Behind the corporeal appearance Plato senses the incorporeal, transcendent, pure Idea. Behind the corrupted creation, under sentence of death, the Christian sees the future creation brought into being by the resurrection, just as God willed it. The contrast, for the Christian, is not between the body and the soul, not between outward form and Idea, but rather between the creation delivered over to death by sin and new creation; between the corruptible, fleshly body and the incorruptible resurrection body.

This leads us to a further point: the Christian interpretation of man. The anthropology of the New Testament is not Greek, but is connected with Jewish conceptions. For the concepts of body, soul, flesh, and spirit (to name only these), the New Testament does indeed use the same words as the Greek philosopher. But they mean something quite different, and we understand the whole New Testament amiss when we construe these concepts only from the point of view of Greek thought. Many misunderstandings arise thus. I cannot present here a biblical anthropology in detail. There are good monographs on the subject,[14] not to mention the appropriate articles in the *Theologisches Wörterbuch*. A complete study would have to treat separately the anthropologies of the various New Testament authors, since on this point there exist differences which are by no means unimportant.[15] Of necessity I can deal here only with a few cardinal points which concern our problem, and even this must be done somewhat schematically, without taking into account the nuances which would have to be discussed in a proper anthropology. In so doing, we shall naturally have

---

[14] W. G. Kümmel, *Das Bild des Menschen im Neuen Testament* (1948).

[15] Also the various theologies of the New Testament should here be mentioned.

to rely primarily upon Paul, since only in his writings do
we find an anthropology which is definable in detail, even
though he too fails to use the different ideas with complete consistency.[16]

The New Testament certainly knows the difference between body and soul, or more precisely, between the inner
and the outer man. This distinction does not, however, im-
ply opposition, as if the one were by nature good, the other by nature bad.[17] Both belong together, both are created
by God. The inner man without the outer has no proper,
full existence. It requires a body. It can, to be sure,
somehow lead a shady existence without the body, like the
dead in Sheol according to the Old Testament, but that is
not a *genuine life*. The contrast with the Greek soul is
clear: it is precisely apart from the body that the Greek
soul attains to full development of its life. According to
the Christian view, however, it is the inner man's very nature which demands the body.

And what now is the role played by the flesh ($\sigma\acute{\alpha}\rho\xi$)
and spirit ($\pi\nu\epsilon\hat{\upsilon}\mu\alpha$)? Here it is especially important not
to be misled by the secular use of the Greek words, though
it is found in various places even in the New Testament and
even within individual writers whose use of terminology is
never completely uniform. With these reservations, we may
say that according to the use which is characteristic, say,
for Pauline theology, flesh and spirit in the New Testament
are two *transcendent* powers which can enter into man from
without; but *neither is given with human existence as such*.
On the whole it is true that the Pauline anthropology, contrary to the Greek, is grounded in *Heilsgeschichte*.[18]

---

[16]W. Gutbrod, *Die paulinische Anthropologie* (1934); W. G.
Kümmel, *Römer 7 und die Bekehrung des Paulus* (1929); E.
Schweitzer, 'Rom. 1:3 f und der Gegensatz von Fleisch und
Geist vor und bei Paulus': *Evang. Theol., 15* (1955), pp.
563 ff; and especially the relevant chapter in R. Bult-
mann, *Theology of the New Testament* (1955).

[17]Also the words of Jesus in Mark 8:36, Matthew 6:25 and
Matthew 10:28 ($\psi\upsilon\chi\acute{\eta}$ = life) do not speak of an 'infinite
value of the immortal soul' and presuppose no higher valu-
ation of the inner man. See also Kümmel, *Das Bild des
Menschen*, pp. 16 ff (also *re* Mark 14:33).

[18]This is what Kümmel, *Das Bild des Menschen*, means when
he states that in the New Testament, including the Johannine theology, man is always conceived as an *historical*
being.

'Flesh' is the power of sin or the power of death. It
seizes the outer and the inner man *together*. *Spirit*
($\pi\nu\epsilon\hat{v}\mu\alpha$) is its great antagonist: the power of creation.
It also seizes the outer and inner man *together*. Flesh and
spirit are active powers, and as such they work within us.
The flesh, the power of death, entered man with the sin of
Adam; indeed it entered the whole man, inner and outer; yet
in such a way that it is very closely linked with the body.
The inner man finds itself less closely connected with the
flesh[19]; although through guilt this power of death has
more and more taken possession even of the inner man. The
spirit, on the other hand, is the great power of life, the
element of the resurrection; God's power of creation is
given to us through the Holy Spirit. In the Old Testament
the Spirit is at work only from time to time in the proph-
ets. In the End-time in which we live—that is, since
Christ has broken the power of death in His own death and
has arisen—this power of life is at work in all members of
the community (Acts 2:16: 'in the last days'). Like the
flesh, it too already takes possession of the whole man,
inner and outer. But whereas, in this age, the flesh has
established itself to a substantial degree in the body,
though it does not rule the inner man in the same ines-
capable way, the quickening power of the Holy Spirit is
already taking possession of the inner man so decisively
that the inner man is 'renewed from day to day', as Paul
says (2 Corinthians 4:16). The whole Johannine Gospel emphasizes the point. We are already in the state of resurrection, that of eternal life—not immortality of soul: the
new era is already inaugurated. The body, too, is already
in the power of the Holy Spirit.

   Wherever the Holy Spirit is at work we have what
amounts to a momentary retreat of the power of death, a
certain foretaste of the End.[20] This is true even in the
body, hence the healings of the sick. But here it is a

----

[19]The body is, so to speak, its locus, from which point it
affects the whole man. This explains why Paul is able to
speak of 'body' instead of 'flesh', or conversely 'flesh'
instead of 'body', contrary to his own basic conception,
although this occurs in very few passages. These termino-
logical exceptions do not alter his general view, which is
characterized by a sharp distinction between body and flesh.

[20]See my article, 'La délivrance anticipée du corps humain
d'après le Nouveau Testament', *Hommage et Reconnaissance.
60 e anniversaire de K. Barth* (1946), pp. 31 ff.

question only of a retreat, not of a final transformation
of the body of death into a resurrection body. Even those
whom Jesus raised up in His lifetime will die again, for
they did not receive a resurrection body, the transformation of the fleshly body into a spiritual body does not
take place until the End. Only then will the Holy Spirit's
power of resurrection take such complete possession of the
body that it transforms it in the way it is already trans-
forming the inner man. It is important to see how different the New Testament anthropology is from that of the
Greeks. Body and soul are both originally good in so far
as they are created by God; they are both bad in so far as
the deadly power of the flesh has hold of them. Both can
and must be set free by the quickening power of the Holy
Spirit.

Here, therefore, deliverance consists not in a release
of soul from body but in a release of both from flesh. We
are not released from the body; rather the body itself is
set free. This is made especially clear in the Pauline
Epistles, but it is the interpretation of the whole New
Testament. In this connexion one does not find the differences which are present among the various books on other
points. Even the much-quoted saying of Jesus in Matthew
10:28 in no way presupposes the Greek conception. 'Fear
not them that kill the body, but cannot kill the soul.' It
might seem to presuppose the view that the soul has no need
of the body, but the context of the passage shows that this
is not the case. Jesus does not continue: 'Be afraid of
him who kills the soul'; rather: 'Fear him who can slay
both soul *and* body in Gehenna.' That is, fear God, who is
able to give you over completely to death; to wit, when He
does not resurrect you to life. We shall see, it is true,
that the soul is the starting-point of the resurrection,
since, as we have said, it can already be possessed by the
Holy Spirit in a way quite different from the body. The
Holy Spirit already lives in our inner man. 'By the Holy
Spirit who dwells in you (already)', says Paul in Romans
8:11, 'God will also quicken your mortal bodies.' Therefore, those who kill only the body are not to be feared.
It can be raised from the dead. Moreover, it must be
raised. The soul cannot always remain without a body. And
on the other side we hear in Jesus' saying in Matthew 10:28
that the soul can be killed. The soul is not immortal.
There must be resurrection for both; for since the Fall the
whole man is 'sown corruptible'. For the inner man, thanks
to the transformation by the quickening power of the Holy
Spirit, the resurrection can take place already in this
present life: through the 'renewal from day to day'. The

flesh, however, still maintains its seat in our body. The transformation of the body does not take place until the End, when the whole creation will be made new by the Holy Spirit, when there will be no death and no corruption.

The resurrection of the body, whose substance[21] will no longer be that of the flesh, but that of the Holy Spirit, is only a part of the *whole new creation*. 'We wait for a new heaven *and* a new earth', says 2 Peter 3:13. The Christian hope relates not only to my individual fate, but to the entire creation. Through sin the whole creation has become involved in death. This we hear not only in Genesis, but also in Romans 8:19 ff, where Paul writes that the whole creation[22] from now on waits longingly for deliverance. This deliverance will come when the power of the Holy Spirit transforms all matter, when God in a new act of creation will not *destroy* matter, but set it free from the flesh, from corruptibility. Not eternal Ideas, but concrete objects will then rise anew, in the new, incorruptible life-substance of the Holy Spirit; and among these objects belongs our body as well.

Because resurrection of the body is a new act of creation which embraces everything, it is not an event which begins with each individual death, but only at the *End*. It is not a transition from this world to another world, as is the case of the immortal soul freed from the body; rather it is the transition from the present age to the future. It is tied to the whole process of redemption.

Because there is sin there must be a process of redemption enacted in time. Where sin is regarded as the source of death's lordship over God's creation, there this sin and death must be vanquished together, and there the Holy Spirit, the only power able to conquer death, must win all creatures back to life in a continuous process.

Therefore the Christian belief in the resurrection, as distinct from the Greek belief in immortality, is tied to a *divine total process* implying deliverance. Sin and death must be conquered. *We* cannot do this. *Another* has done it for us; and He was able to do it only in that He betook

---

[21] I use this rather unfortunate term for want of a better. What I mean by it will be clear from the following discussion.

[22] The allusion in verse 20 to the words 'for your sake' of Genesis 3:17, excludes the translation of κτίσις as 'creature' in the sense of man, a translation advocated by E. Brunner and A. Schlatter. See O. Cullmann, *Christ and Time* (1950), p. 103.

himself to the province of death—that is, He himself died
and expiated sin, so that death as the wages of sin is overcome. Christian faith proclaims that Jesus has done this
and that He arose *with* body and soul after He was fully and
really dead. Here God has consummated the miracle of the
new creation expected at the End. Once again He has created life as in the beginning. At this one point, in Jesus
Christ, this has already happened! Resurrection, not only
in the sense of the Holy Spirit's taking possession of the
inner man, but also resurrection of the *body*. This is a
new creation of matter, an incorruptible matter. Nowhere
else in the world is there this new spiritual matter. Nowhere else is there a spiritual body—only here in Christ.

III THE FIRST-BORN FROM THE DEAD

*Between the Resurrection of Christ and
the Destruction of Death*

We must take into account what it meant for the Christians when they proclaimed: Christ is risen from the dead!
Above all we must bear in mind what death meant for them.
We are tempted to associate these powerful affirmations
with the Greek thought of the immortality of the soul, and
in this way to rob them of their content. Christ is risen:
that is, we stand in the new era in which death is conquered, in which corruptibility is no more. For if there
is really *one* spiritual body (not an immortal soul, but a
spiritual body) which has emerged from a fleshly body, then
indeed the power of death is broken. Believers, according
to the conviction of the first Christians, should no longer
die: this was certainly their expectation in the earliest
days. It must have been a problem when they discovered
that Christians continued to die. But even the fact that
men continue to die no longer has the same significance
after the Resurrection of Christ. The fact of death is
robbed of its former significance. Dying is no longer an
expression of the absolute lordship of Death, but only one
of Death's last contentions for lordship. Death cannot put
an end to the great fact that there is *one* risen Body.

We ought to try simply to understand what the first
Christians meant when they spoke of Christ as being the
'first-born from the dead'. However difficult it may be
for us to do so, we must exclude the question whether or
not we can accept this belief. We must also at the very
start leave on one side the question whether Socrates or

the New Testament is right. Otherwise we shall find ourselves continually mixing alien thought-processes with
those of the New Testament. We should for once simply listen to what the New Testament says. Christ the first-born
from the dead! His body the first Resurrection Body, the
first Spiritual Body. Where this conviction is present,
the whole of life and the whole of thought must be influenced by it. The whole thought of the New Testament remains for us a book sealed with seven seals if we do not
read behind every sentence there this other sentence:
Death has already been overcome (death, be it noted, not
the body); there is already a new creation (a new creation,
be it noted, not an immortality which the soul has always
possessed); the resurrection age is already inaugurated.[23]

Granted that it is only inaugurated, but still it is
decisively inaugurated. *Only* inaugurated: for death is at
work, and Christians still die. The disciples experienced
this as the first members of the Christian community died.
This necessarily presented them with a difficult problem.[24]
In 1 Corinthians 11:30 Paul writes that basically death and
sickness should no longer occur. We still die, and still
there is sickness and sin. But the Holy Spirit is already
effective in our world as the power of new creation; He is
already at work visibly in the primitive community in the
diverse manifestations of the Spirit. In my book *Christ
and Time* I have spoken of a tension between present and
future, the tension between 'already fulfilled' and 'not
yet consummated'. This tension belongs *essentially* to the
New Testament and is not introduced as a secondary solution
born of embarrassment,[25] as Albert Schweitzer's disciples

---

[23]If, as the Qumrân fragment most recently published by Al-
legro seems to confirm, the 'teacher of righteousness' of
this sect really was put to death and his return was
awaited, still what most decisively separates this sect
from the original Christian community (apart from the other
differences, for which see my article, 'The Significance of
the Qumrân Texts', *J.B.L.*, 1955, pp. 213 ff) is the absence
in it of faith in a resurrection which has *already* occurred.

[24]See in this regard Ph. H. Menoud, 'La mort d'Ananias et
de Saphira', *Aux sources de la tradition chrétienne. Me-
langes offerts à M. Goguel* (1950), particularly pp. 150 ff.

[25]See particularly F. Buri, 'Das Problem des ausgebliebenen
Parusie', *Schweiz. Theol. Umschau* (1946), pp. 97 ff. See in
addition O. Cullmann, 'Das wahre durch die ausgebliebene
Parusie gestellte neutestamentliche Problem', *Theol.
Zeitschr.* 3 (1947), p. 177 ff; also pp. 428 ff.

and Rudolph Bultmann maintain.[26] This tension is already
present in and with Jesus. He proclaims the Kingdom of God
for the future; but on the other hand, He proclaims that
the Kingdom of God has already broken in, since He Himself
with the Holy Spirit is indeed already repulsing death by
healing the sick and raising the dead (Matthew 12:28,
11:3 ff, Luke 10:13) in anticipation of the victory over
death which He obtains in His own death. Schweitzer is not
right when he sees as the original Christian hope *only* a
hope in the future; nor is C. H. Dodd when he speaks *only*
of realized eschatology; still less Bultmann when he re-
solves the original hope of Jesus and the first Christians
into Existentialism. It belongs to the very stuff of the
New Testament that it thinks in temporal categories, and
this is because the belief that in Christ the resurrection
is achieved is the starting-point of all Christian living
and thinking. When one starts from this principle, then
the chronological tension between 'already fulfilled' and
'not yet consummated' constitutes the *essence* of the Christian faith. Then the metaphor I use in *Christ and Time*
characterizes the whole New Testament situation: the decisive battle has been fought in Christ's death and Resurrection; only V-day is yet to come.

Basically the whole contemporary theological discussion turns upon this question: Is *Easter* the starting-point
of the Christian Church, of its existence, life, and
thought? If so, we are living in an interim time.

In that case, the faith in resurrection of the New
Testament becomes the cardinal point of all Christian belief. Accordingly, the fact that there is a resurrection
body—Christ's body—defines the first Christians' whole
interpretation of time. If Christ is the 'first-born from
the dead', then this means that the End-time is already
present. But it also means that a temporal interval separates the First-born from all other men who are not yet
'born from the dead'. This means then that we live in an
interim time, between Jesus' Resurrection, which has already taken place, and our own, which will not take place
until the End. It also means, moreover, that the quickening Power, the Holy Spirit, is already at work among us.
Therefore Paul designates the Holy Spirit by the same term—
ἀπαρχή, first-fruits (Romans 8:23)—as he uses for Jesus
Himself (1 Corinthians 15:23). There is then already a
foretaste of the resurrection. And indeed in a twofold way:
our inner man is already being renewed from day to day by

---

[26]R. Bultmann, 'History and Eschatology in the New Testament', *New Test. Stud.*, I (1954), pp. 5 ff.

the Holy Spirit (2 Corinthians 4:16; Ephesians 3:16); the
body also has already been laid hold of by the Spirit, although the flesh still has its citadel within it. Wherever
the Holy Spirit appears, the vanquished power of death re-
coils, even in the body. Hence miracles of healing occur
even in our still mortal body. To the despairing cry in
Romans 7:24, 'Who shall deliver me from this body of death?'
the whole New Testament answers: The Holy Spirit!

The foretaste of the End, realized through the Holy
Spirit, becomes most clearly visible in the early Christian
celebration of the breaking of bread. Visible miracles of
the Spirit occur there. There the Spirit tries to break
through the limits of imperfect human language in the speaking with tongues. And there the community passes over into
direct connexion with the Risen One, not only with His soul,
but also with His Resurrection Body. Therefore we hear in
1 Corinthians 10:16: 'The bread we break, is it not communion with the body of Christ?' Here in communion with the
brethren we come nearest to the Resurrection Body of Christ;
and so Paul writes in the following Chapter 11 (a passage
which has received far too little consideration): if this
Lord's Supper were partaken of by all members of the community in a completely worthy manner, then the union with
Jesus' Resurrection Body would be so effective in our own
bodies that even now there would be no more sickness or
death (1 Corinthians 11:28-30)—a singularly bold assert-
tion.[27] Therefore the community is described as the body
of Christ, because here the spiritual body of Christ is
present, because here we come closest to it; here in the
common meal the first disciples at Easter saw Jesus' Resurrection Body, His Spiritual Body.

Yet in spite of the fact that the Holy Spirit is already so powerfully at work, men still die; even after Easter and Pentecost men continue to die as before. Our body
remains mortal and subject to sickness. Its transformation
into the spiritual body does not take place until the whole
creation is formed anew by God. Then only, for the first
time, there will be nothing but Spirit, nothing but the
power of life, for then death will be destroyed with final-
ity. Then there will be a new substance for all things
visible. Instead of the fleshly matter there appears the
spiritual. That is, *instead of corruptible matter there
appears the incorruptible*. The visible and the invisible

---

[27]F. J. Leenhardt's new study, *Ceci est mon corps. Expli-
cation de ces paroles de Jésus-Christ* (1955), is also to be
understood in the light of this.

will be spirit. But let us make no mistake: this is certainly not the Greek sense of bodiless Idea! A new heaven
and a new earth! That is the Christian hope. And then
will our bodies also rise from the dead. Yet not as fleshly bodies, but as spiritual bodies.

The expression which stands in the ancient Greek texts
of the Apostles' Creed is quite certainly not biblical: 'I
believe in the resurrection of the flesh!'[28] Paul could
not say that. Flesh and blood cannot inherit the Kingdom.
Paul believes in the resurrection of the *body*, not of the
flesh. The flesh is the power of death, which must be destroyed. This error in the Greek creed made its entrance
at a time when the biblical terminology had been miscon-
strued in the sense of Greek anthropology. Our body, moreover (not merely our soul), will be raised at the End, when
the quickening power of the Spirit makes all things new,
all things without exception.

An incorruptible body! How are we to conceive this?
Or better, how did the first Christians conceive of it?
Paul says in Philippians 3:21 that at the End Christ will
transform our lowly body into the body of his own glory
($\delta\delta\xi a$), just as in 2 Corinthians 3:18: 'We are being trans-
formed into his own likeness from glory to glory ($\dot{a}\pi\dot{o}$ $\delta\delta\xi\eta\varsigma$
$\epsilon\dot{\iota}\varsigma$ $\delta o\dot{\xi}a\nu$).' This glory ($\delta\delta\xi a$) was conceived by the first
Christians as a sort of light-substance; but this is only
an imperfect comparison. Our language has no word for it.
Once again I refer to Grünewald's painting of the Resurrection. He may have come closest to what Paul understood as
the spiritual body.

IV   THOSE WHO SLEEP

The Holy Spirit and the Intermediate State of the Dead

And now we come to the last question. When does this
transformation of the body take place? No doubt can remain
on this point. The whole New Testament answers, at the *End*,
and this is to be understood literally, that is, in the

---

[28]W. Bieder, 'Auferstehung des Leibes oder des Fleisches?',
Theol. Zeitschrift, I (1945), pp. 105 ff, seeks to explicate
the expression 'resurrection of the flesh' both from the
point of view of biblical theology and of the history of
dogma.

temporal sense. That raises the question of the 'interim
condition' of the dead. Death is indeed already conquered
according to 2 Timothy 1:10: 'Christ has conquered death
and has already brought life and incorruptibility to light.'
The chronological tension which I constantly stress, concerns precisely this central point: death is conquered, but
it will not be abolished until the End. According to 1 Corinthians 15:26, death will be conquered as the *last enemy*.
It is significant that in the Greek the same verb καταργέω[29]
is used to describe both the decisive victory already accomplished and the not-yet-consummated victory at the end.
John's Apocalypse 20:14 describes the victory at the end,
the annihilation of Death: 'Death will be cast into a pool
of fire'; and a few verses farther on it is said, 'Death
will be no more'.

That means, however, that the transformation of the
body does not occur immediately after each individual death.
Here too we must once again guard against any accommodation
to Greek philosophy, if we wish to understand the New Testament doctrine. This is the point where I cannot accept
Karl Barth's position as a simple restatement of the original Christian view, not even his position in the *Church Dogmatics*[30] where it is subtly shaded and comes much nearer[31]

---

[29]Luther translates καταργέω by 'er hat ihm "die Macht
genommen"' in 2 Timothy 1:10, and by 'er wird aufgehoben'
in 1 Corinthians 15:26.

[30]K. Barth, *Die Kirchliche Dogmatik*, II, 1 (1940), pp.
698 ff; III, 2 (1948), pp. 524 ff, 714 ff.

[31]It is another question, of course, whether Barth does not
have the *right* to adduce relationships in this whole matter
which yet lie outside the New Testament circle of vision.
But if so, then this 'going beyond the New Testament'
should perhaps be done consciously and should always be
identified as such with clarity and emphasis, especially
where a constant effort is being made to argue from the
point of view of the Bible, as is the case with Barth. If
this were done, then the inevitable danger which every dog-
matician *must* confront (and here lies the dignity and greatness of his task) would be more clearly recognized: namely,
the danger that he may not remain upon an extension of the
biblical line, but rather interpret the biblical texts primarily *ex post facto*, from the point of view of his 'going
beyond the New Testament'. Precisely because of this clear
recognition of the danger, discussion with the exegete
would be more fruitful.

to New Testament eschatology than in his first writings.[32]
Karl Barth considers it to be the New Testament interpretation that the transformation of the body occurs for everyone immediately after his individual death—as if the dead
were no longer in time. Nevertheless, according to the New
Testament, they *are* still in time. Otherwise, the problem
in 1 Thessalonians 4:13 ff would have no meaning. Here in
fact Paul is concerned to show that at the moment of
Christ's return 'those who are then alive will have no advantage' over those who have died in Christ. Therefore the
dead in Christ are still in time; they, too, are *waiting*.
'How long, oh Lord?' cry the martyrs who are sleeping under
the altar in John's Apocalypse (6:11). Neither the saying
on the Cross, 'Today you will be with me in paradise' (Luke
23:43), the parable of the rich man, where Lazarus is carried directly to Abraham's bosom (Luke 16:22), nor Paul's
saying 'I desire to die and to be with Christ' (Philippians
1:23), proves as is often maintained that the resurrection
of the body takes place immediately after the individual
death.[33] In none of these texts is there so much as a word

---

[32]Especially *The Resurrection of the Dead* (1926).

[33]Also the much-disputed words of Luke 22:43, 'Today you
will be with me in Paradise', belong here. To be sure it
is not impossible, though artificial, to understand σήμερον
as modifying λέγω σοι. The statement is to be understood
in the light of Luke 16:23 and of the late-Jewish conception of 'Paradise' as the place of the blessed (Strack-
Billerbeck, ad. loc.; P. Volz, *Die Eschatologie der jüdi-
schen Gemeinde im neutest. Zeitalter* (2nd Edn, 1934), p.
265). It is certain that Luke 16:23 does not refer to resurrection of the body, and the expectation of the *Parousia*
is in no way supplanted. Such an interpretation is also
decisively rejected by W. G. Kümmel, *Verheissung und Erfül-
lung*, 2nd Edn (1953), p. 67. A certain disparity here
against Pauline theology does exist in so far as Christ
Himself on the day referred to as 'today' has not yet risen,
and therefore the foundation of the condition wherein the
dead are bound up with Christ has not yet been laid. But
in the last analysis the emphasis here is on the fact that
the thief will be *with Christ*. Menoud (*Le sort des trépassés*, p. 45) correctly points out that Jesus' answer must be
understood in relation to the thief's entreaty. The thief
asks Jesus to remember him when He 'comes into His kingdom',
which according to the Jewish view of the Messiah can only
refer to the time when the Messiah *will come* and erect his
kingdom. Jesus does not grant the request, but instead

about the resurrection of the body. Instead, these different images picture the condition of those who die in Christ
before the End—the interim state in which they, as well as
the living, find themselves. All these images express simply a special proximity to Christ, in which those dying in
Christ before the End find themselves. They are 'with
Christ' or 'in paradise' or 'in Abraham's bosom' or, according to Revelation 6:9, 'under the altar'. All these are
simply various images of special nearness to God. But the
most usual image for Paul is: 'They are asleep.'[34] It
would be difficult to dispute that the New Testament reck-
ons with such an interim time for the dead, as well as for
the living, although any sort of speculation upon the state
of the dead in this interim period is lacking here.

The dead in Christ share in the tension of the interim
time.[35] But this means not *only* that they are waiting. It
means that for them, too, something decisive happened with
Jesus' death and Resurrection. For them, too, Easter is
the great turning point (Matthew 27:52). This new situation created by Easter leads us to see at least the possibility of a common bond with Socrates, not with his teaching, but with his own behaviour in the face of death.
Death has lost its horror, its 'sting'. Though it remains
as the last enemy, Death has no longer any final significance. If the Resurrection of Christ were to designate the
great turning-point of the ages only for the living and not

---

[33](cont.) gives the thief more than he asked for: he will
be united *with Jesus* even before the coming of the kingdom.
So understood, *according to their intention*, these words do
not constitute a difficulty for the position maintained
above.

[34]The interpretation which K. Barth *(Die Kirchliche Dogmatik*, III, 2, p. 778) gives of the 'sleeping', as if this
term conveyed only the 'impression' of a peaceful going to
sleep which those surviving have, finds no support in the
New Testament. The expression in the New Testament signifies more, and like the 'repose' in Apocalypse 14:13 refers
to the *condition* of the dead before the Parousia.

[35]The lack of New Testament speculation on this does not
give us the right simply to suppress the 'interim condition'
as such. I do not understand why Protestant theologians
(including Barth) are so afraid of the New Testament position when the New Testament teaches only this much about
the 'interim condition': (1) that it exists, (2) that it already signifies union with Christ (this because of the Holy
Spirit).

for the dead also, then the living would surely have an immense advantage over the dead. For as members of Christ's community the living are indeed even now in possession of the power of the resurrection, the Holy Spirit. It is unthinkable that, according to the early Christian point of view, nothing should be altered for the dead in the period before the End. It is precisely those images used in the New Testament to describe the condition of the dead in Christ which prove that even now, in this interim state of the dead, the Resurrection of Christ—the anticipation of the End—is already effective. They are 'with Christ'.

Particularly in 2 Corinthians 5:1-10 we hear why it is that the dead, although they do not yet have a body and are only 'sleeping', nevertheless are in special proximity to Christ. Paul speaks here of the natural anxiety which even he feels before death, which still maintains its effectiveness. He fears the condition of 'nakedness', as he calls it; that is, the condition of the inner man who has no body. This natural dread of death, therefore, has not disappeared. Paul would like, as he says, to receive a spiritual body in addition, directly ($\grave{\epsilon}\pi\epsilon\nu\delta\acute{\upsilon}\sigma\alpha\sigma\theta\alpha\iota$) while still living, without undergoing death. That is, he would like to be still alive at the time of Christ's return. Here once again we find confirmation of what we said about Jesus' fear of death. But now we see also something *new*: in this same text alongside this natural anxiety about the soul's nakedness stands the great confidence in Christ's proximity, *even in this interim state*. What is there to be afraid of in the fact that such an interim condition still exists? Confidence in Christ's proximity is grounded in the conviction that our inner man is already grasped by the Holy Spirit. Since the time of Christ, we, the living, do indeed have the Holy Spirit. If He is actually within us, He has already transformed our inner man. But, as we have heard, the Holy Spirit is the power of life. Death can do Him no harm. Therefore something is indeed changed for the dead, for those who really die in Christ, i.e. in possession of the Holy Spirit. The horrible abandonment in death, the separation from God, of which we have spoken, no longer exists, precisely because the Holy Spirit does exist. Therefore the New Testament emphasizes that the dead are indeed *with Christ*, and so not abandoned. Thus we understand how it is that, just in 2 Corinthians 5:1 ff, where he mentions the fear of disembodiment in the interim time, Paul describes the Holy Spirit as the 'earnest'.

According to verse 8 of the same chapter, it even appears that the dead are nearer Christ. The 'sleep' seems to draw them even closer: 'We are willing rather to be absent from the body, and to be at home with the Lord.' For

this reason, the apostle can write in Phil. 1:23 that he
longs to die and be with Christ. So then, a man who lacks
the fleshly body is yet nearer Christ than before, if he
has the Holy Spirit. It is the flesh, bound to our earthly
body, which is throughout our life the hindrance to the
Holy Spirit's full development. Death delivers us from
this hindrance even though it is an imperfect state inas-
much as it lacks the resurrection body. Neither in this
passage nor elsewhere is found any more detailed information about this intermediate state in which the inner man,
stripped indeed of its fleshly body but still deprived of
the spiritual body, exists with the Holy Spirit. The apostle limits himself to assuring us that this state, antici-
pating the destiny which is ours once we have received the
Holy Spirit, brings us closer to the final resurrection.

Here we find fear of a bodiless condition associated
with firm confidence that even in this intermediate, tran-
sient condition no separation from Christ supervenes (among
the powers which cannot separate us from the love of God
in Christ is death—Romans 8:38). This fear *and* this confidence are bound together in 2 Corinthians 5, and this
confirms the fact that even the dead share in the present
tension. Confidence predominates, however, for the decision has indeed been made. Death is conquered. The inner
man, divested of the body, is no longer alone; he does not
lead the shadowy existence which the Jews expected and
which cannot be described as life. The inner man, divested
of the body, has already in his lifetime been transformed
by the Holy Spirit, is already grasped by the resurrection
(Romans 6:3 ff, John 3:3 ff), if he *has* already as a living
person really been renewed by the Holy Spirit. Although he
still 'sleeps' and still awaits the resurrection of the
body, which alone will give him full life, the dead Christian *has* the Holy Spirit. Thus, even in this state, death
has lost its terror, although it still exists. And so the
dead who die in the Lord can actually be blessed 'from now
on' (ἀπ' ἄρτι),[36] as the author of the Johannine Apocalypse

---

[36]In view of the places in the New Testament where ἀπ' ἄρτι
can only mean 'from now on' (for instance, John 13:10, and
in view of the good sense which the sentence makes when
ἀπ' ἄρτι is so translated, I continue to subscribe to the
usual translation 'from now on' and see it as modifying
ἀποθνήσκοντες, although many factors support A. Debrunner's
view, *Grammatik des neutest). Griechisch* (1943), Part II,
Appendix, § 12, following A. Fridrichsen's suggestion,
which understands ἀπαρτί as the colloquial Attic word for

says (14:13). What is said in 1 Corinthians 15:54b, 55
pertains also to the dead: 'Death is swallowed up in victory. O death, where is thy victory? O death, where is
thy sting?' So the Apostle in Romans 14 writes: 'Whether
we live or die, we belong to the Lord' (verse 8). Christ
is 'Lord of the living and the dead' (verse 9).

One could ask whether in this fashion we have not been
led back again, in the last analysis, to the Greek doctrine
of immortality, whether the New Testament does not assume,
for the time after Easter, a continuity of the 'inner Man'
of converted people before and after death, so that here,
too, death is presented for all practical purposes only as
a natural 'transition'.[37] There is a sense in which a kind
of *approximation* to the Greek teaching does actually take
place, to the extent that the inner man, who has already
been transformed by the Spirit (Romans 6:3 ff), and consequently made alive, continues to live with Christ in this
transformed state, in the condition of sleep. This continuity is emphasized especially strongly in the Gospel of
John (3:36, 4:14, 6:54, and frequently). Here we observe
at least a certain analogy to the 'immortality of the
soul', but the distinction remains none the less radical.
Further, the condition of the dead in Christ is still imperfect, a state of 'nakedness', as Paul says, of 'sleep',
of waiting for the resurrection of the whole creation, for
the resurrection of the body. On the other hand, death in
the New Testament continues to be the enemy, albeit a de-
feated enemy, who must yet be destroyed. The fact that
even in this state the dead are already living with Christ
does not correspond to the natural essence of the soul.
Rather it is the result of a divine intervention from outside, through the Holy Spirit, who must already have quickened the inner man in earthly life by His miraculous power.

Thus it is still true that the resurrection of the
body is awaited, even in John's Gospel—though now, of
course, with a certainty of victory because the Holy Spirit
already dwells in the inner man. Hence no doubt can arise
any more: since He already dwells in the inner man, He will
certainly transform the body. For the Holy Spirit, this

---

[36](cont.) 'exactly, certainly' and then finds in P:47's
omission of ναί a support for reading ἀπ' ἄρτι as ἀπαρτί,
modifying λέγει τὸ πνεῦμα, not ἀποθνήσκοντες.

[37]We have already spoken above of K. Barth's attempt (which
indeed goes too far) to place a positive valuation in dia-
lectical fashion alongside the negative valuation of death.

quickening power, penetrates everything and knows no barrier. If He is really within a man, then He will quicken
the whole man. So Paul writes in Romans 8:11: 'If the
Spirit dwells in you, then will He who raised Christ Jesus
from the dead call to life your mortal bodies also *through
the Spirit dwelling in you.*' In Philippians 3:21: 'We wait
for the Lord Jesus Christ, who will conform our lowly body
to the body of His glory.' Nothing is said in the New
Testament about the details of the interim conditions. We
hear only this: we are nearer to God.

   We wait, and *the dead* wait. Of course the rhythm of
time may be different for them than for the living; and in
this way the interim-time may be shortened for them. This
does not, indeed, go beyond the New Testament texts and
their exegesis,[38] because this expression *to sleep*, which
is the customary designation in the New Testament of the
'interim condition', draws us to the view that for the dead
another time-consciousness exists, that of 'those who
sleep'. But that does not mean that the dead are not still
in time. Therefore once again we see that the New Testament resurrection hope is different from the Greek belief
in immortality.

CONCLUSION

   On his missionary journeys Paul surely met people who
were unable to believe in his preaching of the resurrection
for the very reason that they believed in the immortality
of the soul. Thus in Athens there was no laughter until
Paul spoke of the resurrection (Acts 17:32). Both the people of whom Paul says (in 1 Thessalonians 4:13) that 'they
have no hope' and those of whom he writes (in 1 Corinthians
15:12) that they do not believe there is a resurrection
from the dead are probably not Epicureans, as we are inclined to believe. Even those who believe in the immortality of the soul do not have *the* hope of which Paul speaks,
the hope which expresses the belief of a divine miracle of
new creation which will embrace everything, every part of
the world created by God. Indeed for the Greeks who believed in the immortality of the soul it may have been harder to accept the Christian preaching of the resurrection
than it was for others. About the year 150 Justin (in his
Dialogue, 80) writes of people, 'who say that there is no

---

[38]Here I follow R. Mehl's suggestion, *Der letzte Feind*,
p. 56.

resurrection from the dead, but that immediately at death
their souls would ascend to heaven'. Here the contrast is
indeed clearly perceived.

The Emperor Marcus Aurelius, the philosopher who belongs with Socrates to the noblest figures of antiquity,
also perceived the contrast. As is well known, he had the
deepest contempt for Christianity. One might think that
the death of the Christian martyrs would have inspired respect in this great Stoic who regarded death with equanim-
ity. But it was just the martyrs' death with which he was
least sympathetic. The alacrity with which the Christians
met their death displeased him.[39] The Stoic departed this
life dispassionately; the Christian martyr on the other
hand died with spirited passion for the cause of Christ,
because he knew that by doing so he stood within a powerful
redemptive process. The first Christian martyr, Stephen,
shows us (Acts 7:55) how very differently death is bested
by him who dies in Christ than by the ancient philosopher:
he sees, it is said, 'the heavens open and Christ standing
at the right hand of God!' He sees Christ, the Conqueror
of Death. With this faith that the death he must undergo
is already conquered by Him who has Himself endured it,
Stephen lets himself be stoned.

The answer to the question, 'Immortality of the soul
or resurrection of the dead in the New Testament', is un-
equivocal. The *teaching* of the great philosophers Socrates
and Plato can in no way be brought into consonance with
that of the New Testament. That their *person*, their *life*,
and their *bearing in death* can none the less be *honoured*
by Christians, the apologists of the second century have
shown. I believe it can also be demonstrated from the New
Testament. But this is a question with which we do not
have to deal here.

---

[39]M. Aurelius, *Med.*, XI, 3. To be sure, as time went on he
more and more gave up the belief in the soul's immortality.

FROM "THEOLOGY AND VERIFICATION"

John Hick

The idea of an eschatological verification of theism can make sense only if the logically prior idea of continued personal existence after death is intelligible. A desultory debate on this topic has been going on for several years in some of the philosophical periodicals. C. I. Lewis has contended that the hypothesis of immortality "is an hypothesis about our own future experience. And our understanding of what would verify it has no lack of clarity."[1] And Morris Schlick agreed, adding, "We must conclude that immortality, in the sense defined [i.e. 'survival after death,' rather than 'never-ending life'], should not be regarded as a 'metaphysical problem,' but is an empirical hypothesis, because it possesses logical verifiability. It could be verified by following the prescription: 'Wait until you die!'"[2] However, others have challenged this conclusion, either on the ground that the phrase "surviving

---

John H. Hick is H. G. Wood Professor of Theology in the University of Birmingham and has taught at Cornell, Princeton Theological Seminary, and Cambridge. His writings include *Faith and Knowledge* (2nd edition, 1966), *Evil and the God of Love* (1966), and *Arguments for the Existence of God* (1970). The passage included here forms part of an influential essay "Theology and Verification" which first appeared in *Theology Today*, Vol. XVII, 1960. It is reprinted here with permission of the author and the journal. The essay argues that the central beliefs of Christian theism are not incapable of verification but are susceptible to verification eschatologically, since they embody expectations that will be shown to be true when Christian predictions about the afterlife are fulfilled.

[1]"Experience and Meaning," *Philosophical Review*, 1934, reprinted in Feigl and Sellars, *Readings in Philosophical Analysis*, 1949, p. 142.

[2]"Meaning and Verification," *Philosophical Review*, 1936, reprinted in Feigl and Sellars, *op cit.*, p. 160.

death" is self-contradictory in ordinary language or, more
substantially, on the ground that the traditional distinction between soul and body cannot be sustained.[3] I should
like to address myself to this latter view. The only self
of which we know, it is said, is the empirical self, the
walking, talking, acting, sleeping individual who lives, it
may be, for some sixty to eighty years and then dies. Mental events and mental characteristics are analyzed into the
modes of behavior and behavioral dispositions of this empirical self. The human being is described as an organism
capable of acting in the "high-level" ways which we characterize as intelligent, thoughtful, humorous, calculating,
and the like. The concept of mind or soul is thus not the
concept of a "ghost in the machine" (to use Gilbert Ryle's
loaded phrase[4]), but of the more flexible and sophisticated
ways in which human beings behave and have it in them to
behave. On this view there is no room for the notion of
soul in distinction from body; and if there is no soul in
distinction from body, there can be no question of the soul
surviving the death of the body. Against this philosophical background the specifically Christian (and also Jewish)
belief in the resurrection of the flesh, or body, in contrast to the Hellenic notion of the survival of a disembodied soul, might be expected to have attracted more attention than it has. For it is consonant with the conception of man as an indissoluble psycho-physical unity, and
yet it also offers the possibility of an empirical meaning
for the idea of "life after death."

  Paul is the chief Biblical expositor of the idea of
the resurrection of the body.[5] His view, as I understand
it, is this. When someone has died he is, apart from any
special divine action, extinct. A human being is by nature
mortal and subject to annihilation by death. But in fact
God, by an act of sovereign power, either sometimes or always resurrects or (better) reconstitutes or recreates him
—not, however, as the identical physical organism that he
was before death, but as a *soma pneumatikon* ("spiritual
body") embodying the dispositional characteristics and

---

[3]E.g. A.G.N. Flew, "Death," *New Essays in Philosophical
Theology*; "Can a Man Witness his own Funeral?" *Hibbert
Journal*, 1956.

[4]*The Concept of Mind*, 1949, which contains an important exposition of the interpretation of "mental" qualities as
characteristics of behavior.

[5]I Cor. 15. [See above—Ed.]

memory traces of the deceased physical organism, and inhabiting an environment with which the *soma pneumatikon* is continuous as the *ante-mortem* body was continuous with our present world. In discussing this notion we may well abandon the word "spiritual," as lacking today any precise established usage, and speak of "resurrection bodies" and of "the resurrection world." The principal questions to be asked concern the relation between the physical world and the resurrection world, and the criteria of personal identity which are operating when it is alleged that a certain inhabitant of the resurrection world is the same person as an individual who once inhabited this world. The first of these questions turns out on investigation to be the more difficult of the two, and I shall take the easier one first.

Let me sketch a very odd possibility (concerning which, however, I wish to emphasize not so much its oddness as its possibility!), and then see how far it can be stretched in the direction of the notion of the resurrection body. In the process of stretching it will become even more odd than it was before; but my aim will be to show that, however odd, it remains within the bounds of the logically possible. This progression will be presented in three pictures, arranged in a self-explanatory order.

First picture: Suppose that at some learned gathering in this country one of the company were suddenly and inexplicably to disappear, and that at the same moment an exact replica of him were suddenly and inexplicably to appear at some comparable meeting in Australia. The person who appears in Australia is exactly similar, as to both bodily and mental characteristics, with the person who disappears in America. There is continuity of memory, complete similarity of bodily features, including even fingerprints, hair and eye coloration and stomach contents, and also of beliefs, habits, and mental propensities. In fact there is everything that would lead us to identify the one who appeared with the one who disappeared, except continuity of occupancy of space. We may suppose, for example, that a deputation of the colleagues of the man who disappeared fly to Australia to interview the replica of him which is reported there, and find that he is in all respects but one exactly as though he had travelled from say, Princeton to Melbourne, by conventional means. The only difference is that he describes how, as he was sitting listening to Dr. Z reading a paper, on blinking his eyes he suddenly found himself sitting in a different room listening to a different paper by an Australian scholar. He asks his colleagues how the meeting had gone after he ceased to be there, and what they had made of his disappearance, and so on. He clearly

thinks of himself as the one who was present with them at
their meeting in the United States. I suggest that faced
with all these circumstances his colleagues would soon, if
not immediately, find themselves thinking of him and treating him as the individual who had so inexplicably disappeared from their midst. We should be extending our normal
use of "same person" in a way which the postulated facts
would both demand and justify if we said that the one who
appears in Australia is the same person as the one who disappears in America. The factors inclining us to identify
them would far outweigh the factors disinclining us to do
this. We should have no reasonable alternative but to extend our usage of "the same person" to cover the strange
new case.

Second picture: Now let us suppose that the event in
America is not a sudden and inexplicable disappearance, and
indeed not a disappearance at all, but a sudden death.
Only, at the moment when the individual dies, a replica of
him as he was at the moment before his death, complete with
memory up to that instant, appears in Australia. Even with
the corpse on our hands, it would still, I suggest, be an
extension of "same person" required and warranted by the
postulated facts, to say that the same person who died has
been miraculously recreated in Australia. The case would
be considerably odder than in the previous picture, because
of the existence of the corpse in America contemporaneously
with the existence of the living person in Australia. But
I submit that, although the oddness of this circumstance
may be stated as strongly as you please, and can indeed
hardly be overstated, yet it does not exceed the bounds of
the logically possible. Once again we must imagine some
of the deceased's colleagues going to Australia to interview the person who has suddenly appeared there. He would
perfectly remember them and their meeting, be interested in
what had happened, and be as amazed and dumbfounded about
it as anyone else; and he would perhaps be worried about
the possible legal complications if he should return to
America to claim his property; and so on. Once again, I
believe, they would soon find themselves thinking of him
and treating him as the same person as the dead Princeton-
ian. Once again the factors inclining us to say that the
one who died and the one who appeared are the same person
would outweigh the factors inclining us to say that they
are different people. Once again we should have to extend
our usage of "the same person" to cover this new case.

Third picture: My third supposal is that the replica,
complete with memory, etc. appears, not in Australia, but
as a resurrection replica in a different world altogether,

a resurrection world inhabited by resurrected persons. This world occupies its own space, distinct from the space with which we are now familiar. That is to say, an object in the resurrection world is not situated at any distance or in any direction from an object in our present world, although each object in either world is spatially related to each other object in the same world.

Mr. X, then, dies. A Mr. X replica, complete with the set of memory traces which Mr. X had at the last moment before his death, comes into existence. It is composed of other material than physical matter, and is located in a resurrection world which does not stand in any spatial relationship with the physical world. Let us leave out of consideration St. Paul's hint that the resurrection body may be as unlike the physical body as is a full grain of wheat from the wheat seed, and consider the simpler picture in which the resurrection body has the same shape as the physical body.[6]

In these circumstances, how does Mr. X know that he has been resurrected or recreated? He remembers dying; or rather he remembers being on what he took to be his deathbed, and becoming progressively weaker until, presumably, he lost consciousness. But how does he know that (to put it Irishly) his "dying" proved fatal; and that he did not, after losing consciousness, begin to recover strength, and has now simply waked up?

The picture is readily enough elaborated to answer this question. Mr. X meets and recognizes a number of relatives and friends and historical personages whom he knows to have died; and from the fact of their presence, and also from their testimony that he has only just now appeared in their world, he is convinced that he has died. Evidences of this kind could mount up to the point at which they are quite as strong as the evidence which, in pictures one and two, convince the individual in question that he has been miraculously translated to Australia. Resurrected persons would be individually no more in doubt about their own identity than we are now, and would be able to identify one another in the same kinds of ways, and with a like degree of assurance, as we do now.

If it be granted that resurrected persons might be able to arrive at a rationally founded conviction that their existence is *post-mortem*, how could they know that the world in which they find themselves is in a different

---

[6]As would seem to be assumed, for example, by Irenaeus (*Adversus Haereses*, Bk. II, Ch. 34, Sec. 1).

space from that in which their physical bodies were? How
could such a one know that he is not in a like situation
with the person in picture number two, who dies in America
and appears as a full-blooded replica in Australia, leaving
his corpse in the U.S.A.—except that now the replica is
situated, not in Australia, but on a planet of some other
star?

It is of course conceivable that the space of the
resurrection world should have properties which are manifestly incompatible with its being a region of physical
space. But on the other hand, it is not of the essence of
the notion of a resurrection world that its space should
have properties different from those of physical space.
And supposing it not to have different properties, it is
not evident that a resurrected individual could learn from
any direct observations that he was not on a planet of some
sun which is at so great a distance from our own sun that
the stellar scenery visible from it is quite unlike that
which we can now see. The grounds that a resurrected person would have for believing that he is in a different
space from physical space (supposing there to be no dis-
cernible difference in spatial properties) would be the
same as the grounds that any of us may have now for believing this concerning resurrected individuals. These grounds
are indirect and consist in all those considerations (*e.g.*,
Luke 16:26) which lead most of those who consider the question to reject as absurd the possibility of, for example,
radio communication or rocket travel between earth and
heaven.

THE RESURRECTION: OBJECTIONS AND ANSWERS

St. Thomas Aquinas

OBJECTIONS AGAINST THE RESURRECTION

[1] There are, of course, some things which seem to be opposed to faith in the resurrection. Thus: in no natural thing does one find that which has been corrupted returning to being with numerical identity; neither does it seem possible to go back again from privation of a thing to possessing it. Accordingly, since things which are corrupted cannot be repeated with an identity in number, nature intends that the thing which is corrupted be preserved with an identity in species by generation. Since, then, man is corrupted by death, and the very body of man resolved even into the primary elements, it does not seem possible for a man with identity in number to be restored to life.

[2] Again, numerical identity is impossible to a thing if one of its essential principles cannot be numerically identical, for, if an essential principle is varied, that essence of the thing is varied by which the thing, as it is, is also one. But what is returned altogether to nothingness cannot be taken up again with numerical identity; this will be the creation of a new thing rather than the restoration of an identical thing. But there seem to

St. Thomas Aquinas (1225-1274), the greatest of the medieval scholastics and a systematic thinker of great continuing influence, argues characteristically that even though the doctrine of the resurrection is a truth that surpasses reason, it is not contrary to it. "Objections Against the Resurrection" and "Solution of the Objections Mentioned" are Chapters 80 and 81 of Book Four of Aquinas' *Summa Contra Gentiles*. The translation printed here is that of Charles J. O'Neil, which forms part of the English version published by Doubleday and Company under the title *On the Truth of the Catholic Faith*, 1957. It is included here with the permission of the translator and publisher.

be several of the essential principles of man returning to
nothingness by his death. And first, to be sure, his very
corporeity and the form of the compound, since the body is
manifestly dissolved. Then, too, a part of the sensitive
soul, and the nutritive, which cannot be without bodily
organs, seem lost. Further, of course, there seems to return to nothingness the humanity itself—which is said to
be the form of the whole—once the soul is separated from
the body. It seems, then, impossible that man should rise
again being identical in number.

[3] Furthermore, what is not continuous seems not to
be numerically identical. And this is manifest not only
in sizes and motions, but even in qualities and forms, for
if, after healing, a man becomes sick and is healed again,
the health which returns will not be the same in number.
Now, clearly, man's being is taken away by death, since
corruption is a change from being to non-being. It is,
then, impossible that man's being be repeated with numerical identity. Then, neither will the man be the same in
number, for things which are the same in number are the
same in being.

[4] If, furthermore, a man's identical body is restored to life, by equal reasoning whatever was in the
man's body ought to be returned to the same man. But on
this something extremely unseemly follows—not only by reason of the beard and the nails and the hair which are
openly removed by daily trimming, but also by reason of
other parts of the body which are covertly resolved by the
action of the natural heat—and if these all are restored
to the man rising again, an unseemly enormity will rise
with him. It seems, then, that man will not rise after
death.

[5] There is more. It happens, occasionally, that
some men feed on human flesh, and they are nourished on
this nutriment only, and those so nourished generate sons.
Therefore, the same flesh is found in many men. But it is
not possible that it should rise in many. And the resurrection does not seem otherwise to be universal and entire if
there is not restored to every man what he has had here.

[6] Again, that which is common to all those existing
in a species seems to be natural to that species. But the
resurrection of man is not natural, for there is not a natural power of man which suffices to do this. Therefore, not
all men will rise in common.

[7] Furthermore, if by Christ we are freed from fault
and from death, which is the effect of sin, it seems that
those alone ought to be freed who had a share in the mysteries of Christ by which they would be freed from sin.

But this is not true of all men. Therefore, not all men
will rise, it seems.

SOLUTION OF THE OBJECTIONS MENTIONED

[1] Now, toward a solution of these difficulties this
consideration is required: God, as was said above,[1] when He
established human nature, granted the human body something
over and above that which was its due in its natural principles: a kind of incorruptibility, namely, by which it was
suitably adapted to its form, with the result that, as the
life of the soul is perpetual, so the body could live per-
petually by the soul.
[2] And this sort of incorruptibility, although not,
of course, natural in its active principle, was somehow
natural in its order to the end; namely, as matter would be
ordered to its natural form, which is the end of the matter.
[3] When the soul, then, outside the order of its
nature, was turned away from God, that disposition was lost
which had been divinely bestowed on the soul's body to make
it proportionally responsive to the soul; and death followed. Death, therefore, is something added as an accident,
so to say, to man through sin, if one considers the estab-
lishment of human nature.
[4] But this accident was taken away by Christ, who
by the merit of His passion our "death by dying did destroy."[2] From this, then, it follows that by the divine
power which gave the body incorruption the body may once
again be restored from death to life.
[5] In this way, then, one must answer the first argument,[3] that the power of nature fails the divine power, as
the power of an instrument fails the principal agent.
Granted, then, that the operation of nature cannot bring it
about that a corrupted body be restored to life, the divine
power can bring it about. The reason nature is unable to
do this is that nature always operates by a form. But what
has a form, already is. When it was corrupted, of course,
it lost the form which was able to be the principle of the
action. Hence, by nature's operation, what was corrupted
cannot be restored with a numerical identity. But the

---

[1]See above, ch. 52.

[2]This appears to be from the Preface of the Mass of Easter
Sunday; see II Tim. 1:10.

[3]See above, ch. 80, para 1.

divine power which produced things in being operates by
nature in such wise that it can without nature produce
nature's effect, as was previously shown.[4]   Hence, since
the divine power remains the same even when things are
corrupted, it can restore the corrupted to integrity.

[6]   What is stated in the second objection,[5] however, cannot be an obstacle to man's ability to rise with
numerical identity.   For none of man's essential principles
yields entirely to nothingness in death, for the rational
soul which is man's form remains after death, as was shown
above[6]; the matter, also, which was subject to such a form
remains in the same dimensions which made it able to be the
individual matter.   Therefore, by conjunction to a soul numerically the same the man will be restored to matter numerically the same.

[7]   Corporeity, however, can be taken in two ways.
In one way, it can be taken as the substantial form of a
body as it is located in the genus of substance.   Thus, the
corporeity of any body is nothing else but its substantial
form; in accord with this it is fixed in genus and species,
and to this the bodily thing owes its having three dimensions.   For there are not different substantial forms in
one and the same thing, by one of which it is placed in the
supreme genus—substance, say; by another in its proximate
genus—body or animal, say; and by another in its species—
say man or horse.   Since, if the first form were to make
the being substance, the following forms would be accruing
to that which already is actually a definite something (*hoc
aliquid*), and subsisting in nature; thus, the later forms
would not make a definite something, but would be in the
subject which is a definite something as accidental forms.
Therefore, corporeity, as the substantial form in man, cannot be other than the rational soul, which requires in its
own matter the possession of three dimensions, for the soul
is the act of a body.   Another way of taking corporeity is
as an accidental form; in accord with this one says a body
is in the genus of quantity.   And corporeity thus is nothing other than the three dimensions which constitute the
character of body.   Therefore, although this corporeity
yields to nothingness when the human body is corrupted, it
cannot, for all that, be an obstacle to the body's rising
with numerical identity; the reason is that corporeity

---

[4]*SCG*, III, ch. 99.

[5]See above, ch. 80, para 2.

[6]*SCG*, II, ch. 79.

taken in the first way does not yield to nothingness, but remains the same.

[8] In the same fashion, also, the form of a compound can be taken in two ways. In one way it is so taken that by form of a compound one understands the substantial form of the compound body. And thus, since there is not in man any other substantial form than the rational soul, as was shown,[7] one will not be able to say that the form of the compound, as it is the substantial form, yields to nothingness when man dies. Taken in a second way, a form of the compound is called that certain quality which is composed and balanced from the mixture of the simple qualities, and stands to the substantial form of the compound body as the simple quality stands to the substantial form of the simple body. Hence, although the form of the compounding when thus stated yields to nothingness, this is not prejudicial to the unity of the body arising.

[9] Thus, also, must one speak of the nutritive part and the sensitive part. For, if by sensitive part and nutritive part one understands those very capacities which are the natural properties of the soul, or, better, of the composite, then, when the body is corrupted, they are corrupted; nonetheless, this is no obstacle to the unity of the one arising. But, if by the parts mentioned the very substance of the sensitive and nutritive soul is understood, each of those parts is identified with the rational soul. For there are not three souls in man, but only one, as was shown in Book II.[8]

[10] But, in speaking of humanity, one should not understand it as a kind of form coming forth from the union of the form to the matter, as though it were really other than each of the two, because, since by the form the matter is made this actual something, as *De anima* II says,[9] that third form following would be not substantial, but accidental. Of course, some say that the form of the part is the same as the form of the whole: it is called form of the part in that it makes the matter actual being, but it is called form of the whole in that it completes the species essentially. In this way, humanity is not really other than the rational soul. Hence, clearly, when the body is corrupted it does not yield to nothingness. But humanity is the essence of man. The essence of a thing, of course,

---

[7]See above, para 7, and *SCG*, II, ch. 57-62.

[8]*SCG*, II, ch. 58.

[9]Aristotle, *De anima*, II, 1 (412a 9).

is what the definition signifies; and the definition of a natural thing does not signify the form alone, but the form and the matter. Therefore, necessarily, humanity signifies something composite of matter and form, just as "man" does. Differently, nevertheless; for "humanity" signifies the essential principles of the species, both formal and material, prescinding from the individual principles. Humanity is used so far as one is a man; one is not a man by reason of having the individual principles, but only by having the essential principles of the species. Humanity, therefore, signifies only the essential principles of the species. Hence, it is signified in the way in which a part is signified. "Man" truly signifies the essential principles of the species, but does not exclude the individuating principles from its signification, for he is called man who has humanity, and this does not shut out the ability to have other things. For this reason, man is signified as a whole is, for it signifies the essential principles actually, but the individuating principles potentially. "Socrates," however, signifies each set of principles actually, just as the genus contains the difference in potency, but the species contains it actually. Hence, it is clear that man returns numerically the same both by reason of the permanence of the rational soul and by reason of the unity of matter.

[11] However, what is said in the third argument[10]— that being is not one because it is not continuous—rests on a false foundation. For, clearly, the being of matter and form is one; matter has no actual being except by form. Nonetheless, in this respect the rational soul differs from other forms. For there is no being of other forms except in their concrete union with matter, since they exceed matter neither in being nor in operation. But the rational soul plainly exceeds matter in its operation, for it has an operation in which no bodily organ takes part; namely, the act of understanding. Hence, its being, also, is not merely in its concrete union with matter. Its being, therefore, which is that of the composite, remains in the soul even when the body is dissolved; when the body is restored in the resurrection, it is returned to the same being which persisted in the soul.

[12] The fourth objection,[11] also, fails to remove the unity of the one who rises. For what is no obstacle to a man's numerical unity while he continues to live manifestly cannot be an obstacle to the unity of one who rises.

---

[10]See above, ch. 80, para 3.

[11]See above, ch. 80, para 4.

But in the body of man, so long as he is alive, it is not with respect to matter that he has the same parts, but with respect to his species. In respect to matter, of course, the parts are in flux, but this is not an obstacle to his being numerically one from the beginning of his life to the end of it. An example of this can be taken from fire: While it continues to burn, it is called numerically one because its species persists, yet wood is consumed and new wood is applied. It is also like this in the human body, for the form and species of its single parts remain continuously through a whole life; the matter of the parts is not only resolved by the action of the natural heat, but is replenished anew by nourishment. Man is not, therefore, numerically different according to his different ages, although not everything which is in him materially in one state is also there in another. In this way, then, this is not a requirement of man's arising with numerical identity: that he should assume again whatever has been in him during the whole time of his life; but he need assume from that matter only what suffices to complete the quantity due, and that especially must be resumed which was more perfectly consistent with the form and species of humanity. But, if something was wanting to the fulfillment of the quantity due, either because one was overtaken by death before nature could bring him to the quantity due or because mutilation perhaps deprived him of some member, the divine power will supply this from another source. This, however, will be no obstacle to the unity of the body of the one rising, for even the work of nature adds to what a boy has from some other source to bring him to his perfect quantity. And this addition does not make him numerically other, for the man is the same in number whether he is boy or adult.

[13] From this it is clear, also, that there is no obstacle to faith in the resurrection—even in the fact that some men eat human flesh, as the fifth objection[12] was maintaining. For it is not necessary, as has just been shown, that whatever has been in man materially rise in him; further, if something is lacking, it can be supplied by the power of God. Therefore, the flesh consumed will rise in him in whom it was first perfected by the rational soul. But in the second man, if he ate not only human flesh, but other food as well, only that will rise in him which came to him materially from the other food, and which will be necessary to restore the quantity due his body. But, if he ate human flesh only, what rises in him will be that which

---

[12]See above, ch. 80, para 5.

he drew from those who generated him, and what is wanting
will be supplied by the Creator's omnipotence. But let it
be that the parents, too, have eaten only human flesh, and
that as a result their seed—which is the superfluity of
nourishment—has been generated from the flesh of others;
the seed, indeed, will rise in him who was generated from
the seed, and in its place there will be supplied in him
whose flesh was eaten something from another source. For
in the resurrection this situation will obtain: If something was materially present in many men, it will rise in
him to whose perfection it belonged more intimately. Accordingly, if something was in one man as the radical seed
from which he was generated, and in another as the superfluity of nourishment, it will rise in him who was generated
therefrom as from seed. If something was in one as perti-
nent to the perfection of the individual, but in another
as assigned to the perfection of the species, it will rise
in him to whom it belonged as perfection of the individual.
Accordingly, seed will arise in the begotten, not in his
generator; the rib of Adam will arise in Eve, not in Adam
in whom it was present as in a principle of nature. But,
if something was in both in the same degree of perfection,
it will rise in him in whom it was the first time.

[14] Now, however, what is said in the sixth objection[13] can be answered from what has been said. Resurrection is natural if one considers its purpose, for it is
natural that the soul be united to the body. But the principle of resurrection is not natural. It is caused by the
divine power alone.

[15] Nor must one deny that there will be a resurrection of all, although not all cleave to Christ by faith,
and are not imbued with His mysteries.[14] For the Son of
God assumed human nature to restore it. Therefore, what is
a defect of nature will be restored in all, and so all will
return from death to life. But the failure of the person
will not be restored except in those who have adhered to
Christ; either by their own act, believing in Him; or at
least through the sacrament of faith.

---

[13]See above, ch. 80, para 6.

[14]See above, ch. 80, para 7.

Part Three The Evidence
of Psychical Research

THE PROBLEM OF LIFE AFTER DEATH

H. H. Price

May I first say, Mr. Chairman, that I regard it as a great honour to have been invited to take part in this Conference? I speak to you as a philosopher who happens to be interested both in religion and in psychical research (like the Neoplatonists long ago). But I am afraid I am going to discuss some questions which it is 'not done' to talk about.

Some of you may have heard a story about Frederick Myers, the most celebrated, perhaps, of all psychical researchers. At a dinner party he asked his neighbour 'What do you think will happen to you after death?' The reply was 'Oh, I suppose I shall inherit eternal bliss; but I do wish you would not talk about such a depressing subject'. The modern reply to such an inquiry would be rather different. Nowadays the subject of life after death is not merely a depressing one. It is something worse. It is a topic which arouses such strong and uncomfortable emotions that we prefer not to mention it at all. Therefore I address you this afternoon with no little fear and trembling. I am going to talk about what psychical researchers call 'the Problem of Survival'.

In the past 80 years or so, a good deal of evidence has accumulated which is relevant to this problem. Most of it comes from mediumistic communications. Some apparitional phenomena may be relevant as well, and also some of the strange experiences which psychical researchers call 'out-of-the-body experiences'. But I shall talk mainly about mediumistic communications. I shall not say anything about *physical* mediumship, in which such phenomena as telekinesis and materialisation purport to occur. I shall only talk

This paper was first read to a meeting of the Society for the Study of Theology at a conference at Nottingham in April 1967, with Professor H. D. Lewis in the Chair. It was published in *Religious Studies*, Vol. 3, 1968, pp. 447-459. It is reprinted here with the permission of the author and the publisher, Cambridge University Press.

about *mental* mediumship, the sort in which verbal communications are given, either orally or in the form of automatic
writing. These communications can be divided roughly into
two kinds. First, there are those which claim to give us
evidence for survival, that is, for the continued existence
of human personality after bodily death. And secondly,
there are those which claim to give us descriptions of 'the
other world' (or worlds) in which surviving personalities
are alleged to live. Both sorts of communications raise
problems which are relevant to the philosophy of religion.
And the second sort, the descriptive ones, are very unwel-
come to many religious people. If I have time to say anything about them in this paper or in the discussion afterwards, my fear and trembling will be greater than ever.
But obviously one must consider the evidential communications first, because you might very well ask why we should
pay any attention to mediumistic communications at all.

EXTRA-SENSORY PERCEPTIONS

In order to understand what is happening in the very
strange phenomena of mental mediumship one must first consider what is called 'extra-sensory perception' (ESP for
short)—telepathy, clairvoyance, precognition and retrocognition. Extra-sensory perception is the best-established
of all paranormal phenomena. I confess I don't think it is
really very like perception, and should prefer the more non-
committal phrase 'paranormal cognition'. But the term ESP
is now so familiar that I shall go on using it.

It has not been possible, so far, to explain ESP by
any kind of radiation hypothesis, and I doubt whether it
ever will be possible unless we first modify our views of
physical space and time in a pretty drastic manner.

We can however say a little about the psychology of
ESP. There seem to be two distinguishable stages in the
ESP process. The first may be called 'reception' and the
second 'emergence'. It would seem that ESP impressions are
first received at an *unconscious* level of the subject's
mind, and that some sort of barrier or censorship has to be
surmounted or circumvented before they can emerge into consciousness. Consequently, they often emerge 'in an oblique
manner' as my SPR colleague Mrs. Rosalind Heywood has put
it. The paranormally-acquired information may only manage
to 'get through' in a symbolic form. Or it itself does not
get through, though some idea closely associated with it
does. Or it is mixed in among other items which have a normal as opposed to a paranormal origin (as a traveller might

elude the vigilance of the customs officials by mixing
in some prohibited articles among a lot of other innocent
ones). Or again, the paranormally acquired bit of information manages to slip into the margin of consciousness but
not into the focus, and therefore is easily overlooked and
quickly forgotten. Sometimes, again, it emerges in the
form of bodily behaviour, as in automatic writing or the
semi-automatic speech which occurs in some forms of the
mediumistic trance. If as we manage to solve the problem
of bringing our ESP powers under voluntary control (for I
suspect that we all have them in some degree) I think we
shall have to do it by 'smoothing the passage', as it were,
between the unconscious level of our personalities and the
conscious level. The curious practices which diviners and
other psychic persons in all ages have used were probably
designed for this purpose and may not be quite so silly as
they look.

I hope that these sketchy remarks about the nature of
ESP, and especially about its two-stage character (first
unconscious reception and then emergence) may throw some
light on the difficult problems which we now have to discuss.

CONTROLS AND COMMUNICATORS

The phenomena of mental mediumship are both puzzling
and complex. They also vary considerably from one medium
to another; for instance, some go into a deep trance, while
others are only in a slightly dissociated state, not very
far removed from normal waking consciousness.

But most trance mediums purport to have a 'controlling
spirit', usually called 'a control' for short, and some
have more than one. It is important to distinguish between
the control on the one hand, and the communicators on the
other. The control is a kind of master of ceremonies,
whose function is to introduce the communicators and to
look after the medium. It is his task to open the séance
and to bring it to an end when the medium has had enough.
The control usually claims to be the 'spirit' of a deceased
human being, but seldom or never gives much evidence to
support this claim. It seems very likely that the control
is a secondary personality of the medium herself, some part
or stratum of her personality which is repressed in waking
life. Word-association tests give some support to this
view. It may also be significant that controls sometimes
give themselves high sounding foreign names (Mrs. Garrett
for example has two: Urani and Abdul Latif) and that they

sometimes have a rather childish character, for example Mrs. Leonard's control Feda.

The mediumistic evidence for survival, whatever weight you may attach to it, is provided by the communicators and not by the control, who seems to be just a psychologically-helpful part of the machinery of communication.

Next we must notice that the communicators present themselves in two quite different ways. Usually the medium claims to be seeing them or listening to them. She describes what they look like, and then passes on the information which they give her. She says 'he is showing me such and such a thing' or 'he is telling me so and so'. But with some mediums the communicators occasionally take a more dramatic form, sometimes called 'the direct voice'. It is as if the medium were *possessed* by an alien personality quite different from her normal one, who is somehow able to use her body and speak through her lips. There may even be a succession of such alien personalities. Each posesses the medium's body for a time and then gives way to another quite different one.

I myself have witnessed this phenomenon only once (the medium in this case was male, a Mr. Flint). I will mention two of these 'possessing' personalities. The first announced that he had been a London street-Arab in earthly life. He then proceeded to give a long theological discourse, uttered with almost incredible rapidity. It was an exposition of Adoptionist Christology, exceedingly fluent but not at all convincing. I think I have never listened to a more boring sermon in my life.

Then another quite different personality took over, and for some reason he took a special interest in me. At any rate, he walked over to the place where I was sitting and had a short conversation with me. I say 'he' did so, because that was how it felt at the time. Though the physical organism which walked across the room was of course the medium's own, and the lips through which the words came were his, it never struck me at the time that the person talking to me was Mr. Flint himself. On the contrary, it was like meeting a rather friendly stranger whom one had never met before. The first thing he said to me was 'You know, some of your theories are quite wrong'. I replied that this might well be true. Then he said 'your spectacles are broken'. I opened my spectacle case and showed him that they were not. But an hour or so later, while I was waiting for my train at Paddington, I happened to meet an Oxford colleague of mine, who told me that he had broken *his* spectacles. He was much concerned about it, and on the way back to Oxford we spent a considerable time trying to repair them with pipe-cleaners.

I mention this to show how very life-like these 'possessing' personalities can be and how they can apparently have telepathic or precognitive capacities. For though my own spectacles were not broken, a quite unexpected incident concerning broken spectacles did happen to me shortly afterwards. But however impressive this 'possessive' type of mediumship can be, just as a phenomenon, from the *evidential* point of view it is neither better nor worse than the more usual type, in which the medium merely claims to be passing on what he or she has been told (or shown) by the communicator. From the evidential point of view, the crucial question is just this: do we ever find, in either sort of communication, that verifiable information is given concerning the earthly life of the alleged communicator, information which is sufficient to *identify* him with a particular deceased human being?

But first we must make sure that the medium could not have acquired the information in any normal manner (for instance by looking up an old copy of *Who's Who*). We must also make sure that the sitters do not give anything away, either orally or otherwise. For example, it would be unfortunate if one of them were wearing widow's weeds. To avoid such difficulties, we can make use of 'proxy' sitters who were not personally acquainted with the deceased person. Or again, if someone is 'booking' a sitting with a medium, he himself can give an assumed name instead of his real one.

But even though verifiable information is quite often given concerning the earthly career of a particular deceased person, and even though we can often be sure that the medium has not acquired this information in any normal manner, might she not have acquired it by means of her own powers of extra-sensory perception? *Some* paranormal hypothesis seems to be needed, if we are to explain the facts. But need it be the survival hypothesis? This is the most important question we have to ask when we consider the phenomena of mental mediumship, and it is a very difficult question indeed.

To show how difficult it is, I shall make a few remarks about a celebrated case, called the Edgar Vandy case. You will find a full account of it in Professor C. D. Broad's *Lectures on Psychical Research* ch. 15, and a briefer and more popular one in a recent book by Mr. Andrew Mackenzie called *The unexplained*, ch. 11.

THE EDGAR VANDY CASE

A young man called Edgar Vandy died in a drowning accident in August 1933. It was not clear how exactly the accident had happened. So his brother George Vandy had a number of sittings with several mediums in the hope of finding out. (When he arranged the sittings he gave himself a false name and also a false address.) The mystery was never completely cleared up, but some interesting information was given. For instance, at one of the sittings the medium said 'I get the letter H. He is wearing something belonging to your brother who has passed over'. She added 'He (the communicator) is persistent about it. Check it up'. So George Vandy did so; and it turned out that another brother, Harold Vandy, had inadvertently taken and worn Edgar's hat a day or two after Edgar's death.

On another occasion, the medium said that Edgar was showing her a cigarette case, and added 'And that's funny, because he did not smoke'. It was true that Edgar did not smoke, and therefore it seemed very unlikely that he possessed a cigarette case. But the medium gave directions about the place where the cigarette case was. A search was made in the place she described (a certain chest of drawers) and right at the bottom of a drawer, underneath some folded clothes, there was 'a new aluminium box which when held in the hand looked exactly like a metal cigarette case'.

We do have to admit that verifiable information is quite often given in such communications, and we do have to admit (as in the Vandy case which I have just quoted) that it is quite often information which the medium could not have acquired in any normal manner.

How are we to explain such communications? The Survival Hypothesis is one way of explaining them. If the personality of Edgar Vandy did continue to exist after his death he might have found out about the hat in some telepathic or clairvoyant manner, and he might remember about the aluminium box at the bottom of the drawer. He also gave particulars about a drawing of a complicated machine designed by himself, which the medium could not understand at all. If he did survive death, he might be expected to remember about this too.

As I have said, the mystery about his death was never completely cleared up, though several different mediums were consulted. But in a way this apparent failure is consistent with the survival hypothesis and even supports it. At one of the earlier sittings the medium had said 'He is not terribly keen on this enquiry, He does not want you to enquire too closely into the cause of his death'. At a later sitting the medium said 'He was not alone—there was somebody near him who swam away and did not want to help him.' And according to the medium, Edgar added 'I do not altogether blame him'. This suggests that the surviving personality of Edgar Vandy *was* communicating and was trying to shield this other person and save him from getting into trouble.

THE SUPER-ESP HYPOTHESIS

But there is an alternative hypothesis. It is sometimes called the Super-ESP hypothesis. A medium, on this view, is not a person who is capable of getting in touch with inhabitants of another world. She is a person who has very extensive powers of extra-sensory perception. After all, anything which is verifiable in her communications must from the nature of the case be concerned with facts about *this* world. The ostensible communicator may also tell us about the kind of life he claims to be living in the next world and what sort of a world it is. Indeed, we are told a good deal on this subject in some mediumistic communications, both in spoken communications and in automatic scripts. But surely it is obvious that we have no way of 'checking' communications of this other-worldly kind? We can neither verify them nor falsify them. Therefore (it is argued) we must just disregard them altogether, on the ground that they are 'non-evidential'. At the most, they can only throw light on the psychology of the medium in the way that dreams and fantasies do. So we must fix our attention on the evidential communications, those which concern events in *this* world, whether past, present or future.

Since some of them are in fact verified and the information cannot have been acquired in any normal manner, we must try to explain how they come to be made. This is what the Super ESP hypothesis undertakes to do. (Some continental writers call it 'the Animistic hypothesis'. I find this terminology confusing, since the world 'Animism' also has another, quite different sense. The term has long been used to denote the belief—alleged to be held by primitive peoples—that inorganic objects, such as stones or rivers, are alive or 'have souls'.)

Indeed, the Super ESP hypothesis offers us a complete theory of mediumship, and a very plausible one. We know from other evidence (including experimental evidence) that paranormal cognitive capacities—telepathy, clairvoyance, precognition and retrocognition—do exist in a number of human beings. All the verifiable information which a medium

gives us, about the earthly life of a particular deceased
person, and also sometimes about the affairs of his still-
living relatives, including things which are going to happen to them in the future—all this information might conceivably have been acquired by means of the ESP powers of
the medium herself. Let us assume that it *was* acquired in
that way, at an unconscious level of the medium's mind.
The only other assumption we need is that the information
acquired is then (as it were) 'worked up' by a process of
unconscious imaginative dramatisation, and is presented to
the sitters in the form of a more or less plausible impersonation of the deceased relative or friend about whom they
are enquiring.

But indeed it is not just an assumption that the human
mind has these powers of imaginative dramatisation. We may
have to suppose that mediums are more gifted in this respect than most of us. But such powers of imaginative
dramatisation are shown in all of us when we are dreaming
(also, to a lesser extent, in our waking fantasies).

I think we do not sufficiently consider what an ex-
traordinary phenomenon dreaming is. Even the most common-
place and matter-of-fact person shows an astonishing power
of imaginative dramatisation in his dreams. And it seems
to me that there really is a close analogy between mediumistic phenomena and dreaming. The medium is as it were
'dreaming aloud' when she utters her communications. We
must remember in this connection that spontaneous cases of
telepathy occur sometimes in dreams. Indeed, the telepathic dream is perhaps the best known of all types of paranormal phenomena. Dreams are sometimes precognitive too.

If the paranormal cognitive powers of the medium are
extensive and her powers of imaginative dramatisation are
sufficiently great, there is no reason why she should not
present to us a quite recognisable 'impersonation' of a
particular deceased person whom we knew. We can do this
for ourselves when we dream about him. But we get the materials for our imaginative construct from our own memories,
whereas she gets them by means of her ESP powers.

PSEUDO-COMMUNICATORS

The Super ESP hypothesis is also able to explain an
awkward fact which I have not hitherto mentioned. There
are cases of pseudo-communicators. The most famous example
is a purely fictitious character who called himself 'John
Ferguson' and purported to give communications about his
earthly life. The sitter was the well-known psychical re-
searcher Dr. S. G. Soal.

Moreover there is another case, also reported by Dr. Soal, which is even more peculiar. A man called Gordon Davis had been a friend of Dr. Soal's in his youth and Soal believed him to be dead, having heard that he was killed in the first world-war. At a sitting in 1922, Gordon Davis was the communicator. He gave a number of correct details about his schooldays and also about the period when he and Soal had been cadets in the army. Moreover, he spoke with a voice and accent resembling Davis's (it was what is called a 'direct-voice' seance). But it turned out later that Gordon Davis was still alive and was practising as an estate agent in Southend. At the time of the sitting he was interviewing a client.

A believer in the Survival Hypothesis might point out that there are *apparitions* of the living as well as of the dead. But if this analogy is valid, one would expect that mediumistic communications for the living would be more frequent than they are. There are a good many cases of apparitions of the living: but the Gordon Davis case is almost if not quite unique.

You will remember that at an earlier stage of the discussion I distinguished between 'controls' and 'communicators'; and I suggested, in agreement with the majority of psychical researchers, that the control is not a discarnate entity (though it usually claims to be) but is a secondary personality of the medium herself. Its habitat, so to speak, is not the next world, but some unconscious stratum of the medium's own mind. But according to the Super ESP hypothesis, communicators have much the same status as controls have. Both alike are imaginative constructs. The difference between them, according to the Super ESP hypothesis, is only this:—the materials out of which a communicator is constructed get *into* the medium's unconscious in a telepathic or clairvoyant or precognitive manner; whereas the materials out of which a control is constructed are just repressed and perhaps childish wishes, memories and thoughts of her own.

This is the one point on which the Super ESP theory of mediumship agrees with the Spiritualist theory. For the Spiritualists too assign the same status to the control and the communicators: they hold that both alike are discarnate spirits. It is a curious meeting of extremes.

SUPER-ESP VERSUS SURVIVAL

How are we to decide between the Super ESP hypothesis and the survival hypothesis? *Is* there any way of deciding between them? Well, we can say this at any rate. If we

accept the Super ESP hypothesis we do have to suppose that
some living human beings have ESP powers of almost unlimited scope—telepathic, clairvoyant, precognitive and
retrocognitive capacities much greater than our *other* evidence about those capacities would suggest.

Let us consider a sitting at which information is re-
quested concerning a particular deceased person Mr. A. And
let us suppose that it is a proxy sitting: that is, no person who is present at the sitting is a relation or friend
or even acquaintance of the late Mr. A. All the medium is
told is Mr. A's name, and the date and possibly also the
place of his death.

No doubt there are living human beings who know a number of facts about the earthly career of the late Mr. A.
There may also be *documentary* evidence of various kinds
about him (for example letters which he wrote when alive,
obituary notices about him in newspapers). But how does
the medium—or her unconscious—manage to get in touch with
just these people among all the millions of living human
beings that there are? Or if she is to exercise her clairvoyant powers upon those letters or other documents, how is
she to *select* them from among the tons and tons of written
material which exist? Does she, so to speak, follow a telepathic link from the sitter, who is just a proxy, to the absent friends or relatives of the late Mr. A, and then proceed to 'tap' those memories of this deceased person, and
also perhaps their memories concerning the whereabouts of
documents written by him or about him? I do not think we
have much other evidence to suggest that this sort of thing
can be done even by very gifted ESP subjects; and it will
of course have to be done unconsciously if the Super ESP
hypothesis is correct.

COSMIC MEMORY

Similar difficulties arise if we try to bolster up the
Super ESP hypothesis by postulating a 'cosmic memory' in
which every event (or every human event) which ever happens
is somehow retained: something like the 'Great Book' which
we are told of in traditional descriptions of the Day of
Judgement. (You will recall the splendid stanzas about it
in the hymn *Dies Irae*.) For here too the medium suffers
from a kind of *embarras de richesse*. The Great Book may,
somehow, be available to her, but how is she to find the
right page and the right paragraph? It is a very volumi-
nous work indeed!

Moreover, much of what is said about imaginative dramatisation in the Super ESP hypothesis could quite well be accepted by a believer in the Survival Hypothesis. On either of these two hypotheses, we can admit that information acquired in a telepathic manner, at some unconscious level of the medium's mind, *presents* itself in a dramatised form in her utterances. Her remarks 'he is telling me this,' 'he is showing me that' need not be taken to mean that 'he' is literally there beside her. She may indeed have interior mental images—visual images—which make it natural for her to speak in this way. But we may quite well suppose (as I have suggested already) that she is dreaming aloud, as it were—experiencing something like a dream and describing it while she has it.

The important question is, where do the *materials* of this dream come from, since in the course of her dreaming aloud she manages to give correct information which she could not have acquired in any normal manner. If she got them by telepathy, who was the telepathic agent? In the Gordon Davis case he turned out to be a living and physically-embodied human being. When the communicator is wholly fictitious, as in the John Ferguson case, the telepathic agent was presumably the sitter, Dr. Soal. It is not at all uncommon for a medium to 'pick up' thoughts from the minds of the sitters.

Or if the word 'agent' is misleading (because it may suggest that telepathy is a more conscious and more voluntary process than it actually is) let us ask, who or what was the source of this telepathically-acquired information? Once the medium has got the information, she herself (or her unconscious) may proceed to use it as material for a piece of elaborate imaginative dramatisation. But where did she get the information from? This question still remains on our hands, even though we accept all that has been suggested concerning the part which imaginative dramatisation plays in mediumship. And it seems to me that in some cases (the Edgar Vandy case, for instance) much the simplest answer is that she gets the information from the surviving mind of some physically-deceased person, and that some part, at least, of his personality does continue to exist after his physical organism is dead.

The communicator, as he presents himself to us through the medium's utterances, might still be wholly or partly a 'construct' produced by the medium's own mind. And yet telepathy from a discarnate source might provide some, or much, or even most of the materials out of which this imaginative construct is built up. Professor Hornell Hart has

used the analogy of a historical novel to illustrate this
idea. A historical novel is a product of imaginative dramatisation (and much of the work of composing it may well be
done at an unconscious level of the writer's mind). Yet
quite a lot of perfectly good historical fact enters into
this imaginative construct. Some of the characters in the
book are wholly fictitious. But others are not. They really existed and really did, or said, or suffered the things
the novelist describes. And some parts of the story are
betwixt and between. For instance in Scott's picture of
King James I in *The Fortunes of Nigel* there is much genuine
historical material; but some of the incidents and most of
the conversations were the product of the writer's own imaginative powers.

SURVIVAL OF MEMORIES ONLY?

But even though we do think that the Survival hypothesis is the simplest explanation of some mediumistic communications, what kind of survival do they point to? Is it
personal survival? Or does the evidence only suggest that
some or many of the late Mr. A's memories continue to exist
after his physical organism had died? In that case, what
survives would be something less than a person. It was
said of the Bourbons that they had 'learned nothing and
forgotten nothing' during their period of exile after the
French Revolution. If this had been a complete description
of their mental life in that period, they must have ceased
to be *persons* for 24 years or so, and only began to be persons again when they returned to France in 1814. (This may
suggest a rather repulsive version of the Reincarnation theory, which I leave you to work out for yourselves.) For
genuinely personal survival, we need evidence of something
more than mere survival of memories. We need evidence of
continuing mental activity of a purposive kind.

Do we get it? On the face of it, we sometimes do. In
the Edgar Vandy case already quoted, it looks as if the communicator was trying to produce evidence which would identify him. Moreover (and more important perhaps) it looks
as if he was trying to prevent his relatives from finding
out just why he was not rescued, and trying—successfully—
to shield or protect the person responsible. As you will
remember, he was represented as saying 'He does not want
you to enquire too closely into the causes of his death'.

I will now mention another case, a non-mediumistic one,
which seems to show evidence of purpose. It is the Chaffin
Will case. Mr. Chaffin, a farmer in North Carolina, died

in 1921. He left a will, dated 1905, in which the whole of
his property was left to one of his four sons, Marshall
Chaffin. Some four years later another son, James, began
to have vivid dreams in which his father appeared at his
bedside and spoke to him. In one of these (it is not quite
clear whether it was a dream or a half-waking vision) his
father was dressed in an old black overcoat and said 'You
will find my will in my overcoat pocket'. James found the
overcoat and looked inside the pocket which had been sewn
up. Inside was a piece of paper on which was written 'Read
the 27th chapter of *Genesis* in my daddie's old bible'.
(This is the chapter describing how Jacob supplanted Easau.)
James found the old bible in a drawer and between the pages
containing *Genesis* ch. 27 there was another will dated 1919,
14 years later than the first one. In this the testator
said that after reading Genesis ch. 27, he wished his property to be divided equally between his four sons. This
will, though unattested by witnesses, was valid by the laws
of North Carolina, and its provisions were accordingly carried out. Here we do seem to have evidence of *post mortem*
purposive activity.

THE CROSS-CORRESPONDENCES

Moreover, we sometimes seem to have evidence of something more, not only purpose but also of a quite elaborate
intelligent design. The best-known examples of this are
the Cross Correspondence cases investigated by the Society
for Psychical Research in the first quarter of this century.
The story is exceedingly complicated. You will find an
excellent presentation of it in Mr. W. H. Salter's book
Zoar, pp. 169-208. I shall just give you a very brief
sketch of the kind of thing which happened. Most of the
material came in the form of automatic writing. A number
of automatic writers began to produce scripts independently
of each other. The scripts contained many rather recondite
literary allusions, mostly to the Greek and Latin classics;
and when any one script was read by itself, it was impossible to see what the point of the allusions was. But when
several scripts were considered together, it was found that
those cryptic allusions made sense. What automatist A had
written referred to something which automatist B had written independently. Sometimes *directions* were actually giv-
en in the script of one automatist A, telling her to send
her script to another automatist B, someone she had not met.
It does look as if there were evidence of *post mortem*
design here (a very ingenious design too) and it was eventu-

ally claimed in the scripts themselves that the author of
the design was Frederick Myers, who had died shortly before
the Cross-Correspondences began and was himself a very
accomplished classical scholar. If we reject this explanation, we shall have to suppose that a great deal of elaborate and ingenious planning went on in the mind of one of
the automatists, though none of them had any conscious
awareness of any such planning. There must have been a
great deal of unconscious telepathy too, whereby the arch-
planner revealed little bits of the plan (but not too much)
to each of the other participants.

Here we have another illustration of a point which I
tried to make earlier. One may put it like this:—the more
you *deflate* the survival hypothesis, the more you have to
inflate the powers of the human unconscious—the unconscious stratum or level of the minds of physically-embodied
human beings. We have already seen how much they have to
be inflated in the Super ESP hypothesis. And we have to
inflate them still more when we consider the special sort
of evidence presented to us in the Cross-Correspondence
cases.

COMMUNICATIONS DESCRIBING 'OTHER WORLDS'

Finally, there is one other point which has to be considered if we are inclined to think that the mediumistic
evidence for survival will only establish (at the most) the
survival of a set of memories, something much less than the
survival of a complete personality.

There are mediumistic communications which purport to
describe 'the other world' and the kind of life which the
communicator is living in his *post mortem* condition. As I
have said already, some psychical researchers maintain that
communications of this purely descriptive kind should be ignored altogether, on the ground that they are 'non-evidential'. It is of course true that we have no way of verify-
ing them or falsifying them; and it is not much good to
reply 'just wait till you are dead, and then you will be
able to see for yourself whether they are correct or not',
since this obviously begs the question in favour of the Survival Hypothesis. All the same, this recommendation, that
communications of this other-world-describing kind should
just be ignored altogether, seems to me altogether *too* posi-
tivistic and puritanical.

May I remind you of my point about the Bourbons, who
were said to have learned nothing and forgotten nothing?
These so-called non-evidential communications do suggest

that the communicators *have* learned something since they died. We 'live and learn'. Or rather we do not live in a personal way unless we continue to have experiences—new experiences, and not just memories of old ones. Let me put it this way: if the Survival Hypothesis is true, there *ought* to be communications of this purely descriptive kind, describing 'other worlds' and the kind of life which is alleged to be lived in them. And if such descriptive communications never occurred, that would be a very serious objection to the Survival Hypothesis. In fact, however, communications of this other-world-describing kind are very abundant, almost embarrassingly so. Some of these descriptions (not all of them) are tolerably clear and coherent and have at any rate the kind of interest which travellers' tales have. My own knowledge of this kind of mediumistic literature is pretty slight and superficial. All the same I wish I had time to say a little about it, because these other-world-describing communications do raise theological problems. Some of them are very repugnant to religious people (and not without reason). I am afraid there are the beginnings of a kind of conflict between psychical research and religion here; and this distresses me, because I happen to have a foot in both camps.

CONCLUSION

Obviously I have not time to discuss these other-world-descriptions now (I will try to say something about them in the discussion afterwards, if any of you are interested). But now I must try to sum up the main argument of this lecture.

My aim was to show that some mediumistic communications do provide us with *evidence* for the continued existence of human personality after death. I am very far from claiming that this evidence is conclusive. But I think it is strong enough to justify the following piece of advice: 'Do not be too sure that you will *not* continue to exist as a person after your physical organism has died'. And even though we cannot go farther than that, the investigation of mental mediumship has taught us something which is quite important.

THE QUESTION OF SURVIVAL

Antony Flew

> Whether we are to live in a future state, as
> it is the most important question which can possi-
> bly be asked, so it is the most intelligible one
> which can be expressed in language.
> —Bishop Butler,
> *Of Personal Identity*

  In the last chapter we concluded that enough impressive mediumistic mental phenomena had been produced under
sufficiently safeguarded conditions to demand, or at least
to justify, the assumption that some paranormal factor has
sometimes been at work in their production. To put it more
precisely, what is involved is this: some mediums and automatists have given items of true information which they
could not have acquired by any normal means; not even if
they were gifted with hyper-acute senses, masterly powers
of inference, or superlative memory capacity; nor yet with
any combination of these, whether conscious or unconscious.
And these pieces of information have been presented as de-
riving from people who have died. Often they have been
presented in the style, in the voice, and with the mannerisms of those people. Often again they have been things
which those people certainly did know when they were alive.

Antony Flew is Professor of Philosophy in the University of
Reading. He was for many years Professor at the University
of Keele and was recently at The University of Calgary.
His many writings include *Hume's Philosophy of Belief* (1961),
God and Philosophy (1966), *Evolutionary Ethics* (1967), and
Crime and Disease? (1973). He has also edited several well-
known anthologies, including *Logic and Language* (First Series 1951, Second Series 1953) and (with Alasdair MacIntyre)
New Essays in Philosophical Theology (1955). "The Question
of Survival" is Chapter VII of Professor Flew's *A New Approach to Psychical Research*, published by C. A. Watts & Co.,
London, in 1953. It is reprinted here with the permission
of the author and publisher.

Now once it has been admitted or at least supposed for the sake of argument that this information (and the associated characterizations) cannot have been normally acquired (or provided) by the medium or automatist (and of course that it cannot be explained away as consisting only of lucky shots), it might seem that there was no option but to put some sort of spiritualist interpretation on the facts—to say that this information did indeed derive from the spirits of the surviving dead. In this chapter we are going to criticize this interpretation on two levels: first, taking it at its face value, by arguing that even on this level it is not really as simple and as adequate to the facts as at first sight it seems to be; second, by suggesting, albeit extremely sketchily, some of the philosophical difficulties involved in this apparently pellucid notion of personal survival.

Suppose then that we accept for the moment the survivalist interpretation at its face value. It seems natural and straightforward. By contrast, once the presence of any paranormal factor has been conceded, the attempt to describe the phenomena alternatively in terms of the supposed telepathic and/or clairvoyant (and/or possibly even precognitive) powers of the medium or automatist and other living people, must seem strained and far-fetched. But, as was realized early in the history of the S.P.R., and not least acutely by some of those like F.W.H. Myers who were most keen to prove survival, this is a mistake. It seems natural and straightforward to accept it because it is the interpretation which those mediumistic phenomena with which we are most familiar, so to speak, put upon themselves; and because we have not come across any closely parallel phenomena which do not fit in with such an interpretation. But there have been such parallel phenomena. The survivalist account seems simple. But only at first sight: for, quite apart from difficulties of the sort we shall raise in the second half of this chapter, it involves many extra assumptions, mostly unsupported by independent evidence, in addition to those required by the alternative account, which are suggested by independent evidence. It is thus, scientifically speaking, much more elaborate: and *frusta fit per plura quod potest fieri per pauciora*[1] (William of Ockham: *Summa totius logicae*).

---

[1]"It is futile to do with more elements what can be done with fewer": the usual version of Ockham's Razor *Entia non sunt multiplicanda praeter necessitatem* "Entities should not be multiplied unnecessarily" is not to be found in his extant works.

In the Anglo-Saxon countries nowadays mediumistic phenomena always tend to take a spiritualistic form. Information is presented as coming from the "spirits of the surviving dead". The dramatic characterizations are of, and
allegedly by, people who have lived and died "and are now
living on another plane". Putatively paranormal physical
phenomena are offered as signs of the presence and powers
of "spirits" and as an authentication of their supposed communications. But this has certainly not been the case universally and always, and the exceptions are of great theoretical importance. The two groups of pre-nineteenth-
century mediums or quasi-mediums about whom we have most
information, though said to have performed many of the
feats attributed to modern mediums, did not ascribe their
successes to the spirits of the dead. The κάτοχοι of the
later Ancient period perversely gave credit to non-human
gods or dæmons. The witches of the sixteenth and seven-
teenth centuries rashly confessed to assistance from the
devil. Incidentally, it is hard to see what bearing the
occurrence of paranormal physical phenomena would have on
the question of survival. For unless there were reason to
think that death endows a "man" with powers of levitating
toy trumpets and so forth, such a performance could scarcely
even assist in authenticating the claim that messages accom-
panying it originated "on the other side"; any more than—
pace the advertisers and the mass newspapers—prowess in
athletics or motor-racing gives weight to a celebrity's en-
dorsement of a hair-cream or a religion.

In France, where the Spiritualist cult is less widespread than it is in the Anglo-Saxon world, Dr. Osty tested
a subject, Mme. Morel, who produced under his supervision
many true items of information, both about the living and
about the dead, which were comparable in range and in accu-
racy with the work of the best spirit mediums; and the production of which was equally inexplicable in normal terms.
But she did this without benefit of any Controls or Communicators: and did not attribute her successes to spirit aid.
Presumably with a different climate of opinion to mould her
development she would have become an orthodox spirit medium,
and in other environments perhaps a seer or a prophetess or
a "wise woman". (See "Télépathie Spontanée et Transmission
de Pensée Expérimentale" in *Revue Métapsychique*, 1932-3,
pp. 80-3.)

Again, to parallel the proxy sittings, Osty reports
that another of his subjects, Mme. Peyroutel, on being asked
to describe the past life of a living person of whom he was
thinking, gave very distinctive details, which were quite
unknown to Osty, were not normally accessible to her, and

were later confirmed as correct by intimates of the person in question. (*La Connaissance Supernormale*, pp. 148 ff.: this and the previous reference are both borrowed from Professor E. R. Dodds' "Why I do not Believe in Survival," *Proc. S.P.R.*, Vol. XLII, to which and to whom I owe much else besides. It is only fair to add that it does not seem to me that Osty's work, however sound his conclusions, was up to the best S.P.R. standards.)

The vivid characterization by a medium in trance of a person who was never normally known to her can also be curiously paralleled. Dr. S. G. Soal, whose statistical ESP experiments will be mentioned later, reports that at a sitting with Mrs. Blanche Cooper a Communicator calling "himself" Gordon Davis appeared. But later and much to his surprise Soal discovered that his acquaintance Gordon Davis had not, as he had previously believed, been killed in the war. He was still alive and had, at the time of the sittings, been practising as an estate agent in Southend. The voice of "Gordon Davis" was so apparently realistic that Soal exclaimed "By Jove! and it's *like* Gordon Davis too", and the turns of speech were later agreed by both Davis and Soal to be characteristic. Most of the statements made by "Gordon Davis" were later found to fit Gordon Davis. The most remarkable fact was that a description of the internal arrangements of a house given by "him" fitted the actual arrangements of the Davis home, into which he had not moved till a year after the sittings with Mrs. Cooper. ("A Report on some Communications Received through Mrs. Blanche Cooper," *Proc. S.P.R.*, Vol. XXXV; this particular case, pp. 560 ff.)

Even the features of the cross-correspondences, which "Myers" deliberately devised in order to remove or at least to restrict the possibility of a description in terms of the normal and paranormal capacities of the living only, have some parallels which could only be fitted into a spiritualist account very artificially. In many experiments in telepathy the "receiver" seems to be groping near and for the idea the "transmitter" has wished to convey. In one case—the Ramsden-Miles series—when Miss Miles wanted to send *Sphinx*, Miss Ramsden recorded *Luxor in Egypt*, and when she wanted to produce *Bishop*, Miss Ramsden ended *latme, Bishop Latimer, Archbishop*. In another case when a "transmitter" wanted Professor Gilbert Murray to think of *Sir Francis Drake drinking the health of Doughty the mutineer*, what he actually got was a *faint feeling of Arabia or desert*: a neat example of the sort of disguised allusion attributed to Myers.[2] A third case was especially inter-

---

[2]*Arabia Deserta* was written by (another) Doughty.

esting because two of the leading figures of the cross-correspondence work were involved. Dr. A. W. Verrall wanted to infiltrate into his wife's automatic scripts the three Greek words μονόπωλον ἐς ἀῶ (rendered as *One-Horse Dawn*: which gave a name to the case). In the next six months those scripts did in fact give just such a series of groping references as would have been scored as a cross-correspondence if they had been occurring in the products of different automatists. They also had, on different occasions, separate sentences which made sense only when put together. And they even had one of those recondite allusive passages: *Find the herb moly, that will help—it is a clue.* The allusion was later tracked down by Mrs. Verrall to another of the papers set in the Cambridge Classical Tripos in the same year as that from which her husband had culled the three enigmatic Greek words. (See Professor A. C. Pigou in *Proc. S.P.R.*, Vol. XXIII, pp. 286 ff.)

Besides such non-spiritualistic parallels to the marvels of spirit mediumship and automatism, there have been some indications in the work of the best of these mediums and automatists which point in the same direction. *First,* there are cases where erroneous communications seem to be most plausibly described as based on telepathy from the sitter to the medium. In the paper already referred to Soal reports that a "John Ferguson" appeared at sittings with Mrs. Blanche Cooper, claiming to be a brother of a James Ferguson with whom the investigator had been at school. Soal privately invented various hypotheses about this putative John Ferguson. These were duly retailed to him as facts at later sittings. But he was in the meantime able to prove that no such John Ferguson had ever existed. Again at sittings with Mrs. Piper, Hodgson one day thought about Sir Walter Scott. Next day a manifestly fictitious "Sir Walter Scott" communicated. On another occasion when he had at one sitting been thinking of the notorious physical medium D. D. Home, a similarly spurious "D. D. Home" appeared next day.

Second, if we make the assumption that, other things being equal, telepathy is more likely to occur between two people when they are close together than when they are far apart, then some results reported by Mr. H. F. Saltmarsh are suggestive. This assumption has a fair amount of support; though nothing much can be said with assurance about what conditions favour telepathy. Saltmarsh found that in a series of sittings, fifty-three ordinary and eighty-nine proxy, with Mrs. Warren Elliott, the percentage of true statements in the former class was more than double what it was in the latter; while several Communicators who did well in ordinary conditions made no score at all at proxy sittings. ("Report on the Investigation of Some Sittings with Mrs. Warren Elliott," *Proc. S.P.R.*, Vol. XXXIX.) Similar analysis has yet to be applied to the recorded work of other outstanding mediums. But even if Saltmarsh's results were confirmed and supplemented in this way, some story about "the spirits" needing the presence of sympathetic loved ones would still fit the facts.

Third, students of mediumistic communications have frequently commented on their disjointedness. Bits and pieces of information come spasmodically. This is just what would be expected on the theory that the items which are not normally available to the medium are picked up paranormally, and usually unconsciously, from other living people. For in the non-spiritualistic cases of apparent telepathy miscellaneous scraps of information are acquired sporadically. However, in a spiritualist account all this can be ascribed to the difficulties of getting the messages through: and this difficulty is no doubt considerable; or how are we to account for the failure—often remarked by the incredulous—of the spirits to make themselves more widely known before the middle of the last century?

Fourth, no Control or Communicator—however great was the literary ability possessed by his earthly namesake—ever seems able to give a plausible and distinctive account of his present mode of existence. What is offered always looks deplorably like a tawdry product of the medium's phantasy life, moulded by the fashionable doctrines of her culture circle. French spirits are often reincarnationists following Allan Kardec, whereas Anglo-Saxon ones know nothing of any rebirth from the "glorious Summerland".

Fifth—a similar point—the "spirits," even when their namesakes have been active and able people, never give *evidence* either of any development since death or of any private activity between séances: though more than enough is *said* about "deepening understanding," "spiritual growth," and so on, since they "crossed over to the other side."

Now, none of these parallel cases and internal indications rule out a spiritualistic interpretation. Something could be done to allow for all of them separately. But taken together they do make such an account look a great deal less easy and less inevitable. The telepathic (ESP) alternative involves fewer assumptions: only that mediums sometimes show a paranormal faculty for the reality of which there is much other evidence; and that they show it in a degree for which there is some other evidence. The spiritualist account demands, at least, that many human personalities survive death (whatever precisely this may mean)

in addition to the existence of the powers postulated in
the telepathic (ESP) account. If as usually is the case
the spiritualist view is extended to cover successful book-
tests and object-reading,[3] as well as paranormal physical
phenomena, then the telepathic alternative is equally capable of parallel extension. For the further powers which
now have to be attributed to "the spirits" could be ascribed to the medium and other people. In each case there
is evidence pointing to the display by people making no
spiritualist claims of such a paranormal power. (See, for
instance, Chapter VIII for card-guessing under "clairvoyance" conditions and for "psychokinesis" in the laboratory.)
The relative position of the ESP and the spiritualist interpretations—or rather types of interpretation, for there
are many possible species in each genus—will remain the
same.

It is important to emphasize the word "interpretation".
The rival views certainly cannot be awarded the status of
explanations. To say that the paranormal element in a séance is due to telepathy etc. between the various people
concerned is not at all like saying that the co-ordination
of the elements in an armoured division is secured by radio
telephony. "Telepathy" is not the name of a means of communication; whereas the mention of radio telephony does explain how certain results are achieved, by indicating the
mechanisms involved. Telepathy is no more an explanation
of the paranormal element in séance performances than memory is an explanation of our capacity to give our names and
addresses.

In this respect talk of "the spirits" is certainly no
better; in spite of the explanatory pretensions with which
it is often introduced. For on this view "the spirits"
also have to be credited with all the still mysterious
paranormal powers, which the alternative view attributes to
people only. Furthermore, they must possess them to a far
higher degree. For, presumably, bodiless beings could not
either acquire information or convey it, either to one another, or, crucially, to the "spirit controls" manipulating
mediums, except "by ESP". Some spirits have produced information not normally available to their mediums about
things that occurred after the deaths of their namesakes.

---

[3]"Object-reading" or "psychometry," are the names given to
the alleged performance of providing true information about
the history of some object, which could not be inferred by
and has never been known to the psychic.

The postulation of surviving spirits might look plausible if with the progress of research we found that the alternative ESP account would have to attribute to people ESP capacities considerably greater, both than those for which we could find evidence outside spiritist contexts, and than those which the spirit account needed to attribute to spirits. The first condition would not be satisfied if we could then find any reason why mediums and others should put up in spiritualist contexts exceptionally good ESP performances. But it would be if we found that our ESP account would have to attribute to the sitters ESP performances either under conditions which were independently known to be inhibitory, or of which these particular sitters were independently known to be incapable. Once it was easier than it is now to believe that the first condition would be satisfied in this way (see e.g., Hodgson's work on Mrs. Piper, used by Broad in this sense in *The Mind and its Place in Nature*, Kegan Paul 1925, pp. 548 ff.).

The second condition would lose its force if any reason could be given why "surviving spirits" should be better ESP performers than their former namesakes. This difficulty has too often been overlooked. This is presumably partly on the same worthless principle *omne ignotum pro magnifico*[4] which has misled people to think that physical mediumship could give emphatic warrant to "spirit" claims.

Before the postulation was justified a third condition would have to be satisfied: the discovery of good independent reason for saying that memory performances could occur after the dissolution of the brain of which they were normally thought to be a function. This is important, because most of the paranormally provided information in most séances, and with appropriate alterations the same thing applies to characteristic mannerisms, direct voices, etc., is such as some person, as a matter of fact dead, would have been able to give from memory were he still alive and well: hence the desire to describe the séance by reference to the "spirit" of the person in question. But even supposing that the first two conditions are met, the spiritist account is still not going to be more plausible than its rival. What it gains on the ESP side, by not having to allow for huge inexplicable increases in ESP capacity in the single context of the séance, it loses elsewhere by having to postulate a special faculty of brainless memory, possessed by its postulated spirits. This third condition might be satisfied if all the efforts of the neurophysiolo-

---

[4]Freely: "Everything unknown is a miracle".

gists and psychologists failed to account for memory in neurophysiological terms. Those who for any reason hope for this may be encouraged by the confession of K. S. Lashley, one of those who have tried hardest to outline such an account: "I sometimes feel, in reviewing the evidence on the localization of the memory trace, that the necessary conclusion is that learning just is not possible." The rest of us can reflect—with Lashley—that it is early days for despair.

Furthermore, until and unless the concept "spirit" is made a great deal more specific than it is at present, the spirit account cannot serve as a scientific hypothesis. To use it as such we should have to be able to deduce from it definite and testable consequences. We should need to be able to say that, if it were correct, such and such tests would yield such and such results. We cannot, because with the spirits anything goes; nothing is definitely predictable. Or, to put it less misleadingly, the concept of spirit is hopelessly indeterminate. This is the main reason why the word "spirit" has no place in the language of science.

Professor C. D. Broad's psychic factor theory is relevant here. He has suggested, without very firm conviction, that minds might be "a compound of two factors, neither of which separately has the characteristic properties of a mind, just as salt is a compound of two substances neither of which by itself has the characteristic properties of salt. . . . The psychic factor would be like some chemical element which has never been isolated; and the characteristics of a mind would depend jointly on those of the psychic factor and on those of the material organism with which it is united" (*loc. cit.*, pp. 535-6). The analogy to a chemical compound would hold in so far as "chemical compounds have properties which cannot be deduced from those which their elements display in isolation or in other compounds . . . [although] . . . the properties of the compounds are wholly dependent on those of the elements, in the sense that given such elements in such relations, a compound necessarily arises with such and such properties . . . [which] . . . do not belong to the elements, but only to the compound as a whole" (p. 536). But it would break down in so far as when "two chemical elements are united to form a chemical compound no permanent change is produced in the properties of either . . . [whereas] . . . when a psychic factor is united with a bodily organism so as to give a mind both factors may be permanently affected by this union" (p. 536).

This sort of view has two signal superiorities over spiritisms. First: while the word "spirit" combines the minimum of determinate meaning with the maximum of emotive disturbance, the new term "psychic factor" can be given precisely as much and what meaning we wish, and so far is sterile emotionally. Broad was only willing to commit himself to the chemical analogy; and to insisting that "it is capable of carrying traces of past experiences and of certain personal peculiarities" (p. 659). Second: psychic factors, unlike spirits, could not be expected either to retain all the mental capacities of their mortal namesakes or to enjoy any private life and development between séances when they are not married to any bodily factor. This squares with their "singular reticence about their present life, characters, and surroundings" (p. 540).

But, after allowing for these advantages, this view is surely open to criticisms similar to those deployed against spiritisms. It is—as Broad of course saw (p. 538)—more complex than its ESP rival. For it postulates a new class of entities, psychic factors, and attributes to them that capacity of carrying memory traces which is usually considered the prerogative of the brain. Broad's psychic factors will have to be endowed with much the same ESP capacities as the rival interpretation has to attribute to people. When Broad originally developed this view it did have compensating advantages. For he was writing before both the great advances in laboratory ESP and the publication of much further work on mediumship suggesting that psychic factors would have to be credited with considerable ESP powers as well as the possession of many memory traces appropriate to their dead namesakes. But the former have made it seem that we shall have in any case to credit some people with considerable ESP capacity. The latter have indicated that even psychic factors—which, unlike spirits, do not have private lives apart from séances, and so do not have to be credited with enormous ESP powers on that account—would have to be conceded considerable ones. The Communicators of entranced mediums sometimes produce information which was not normally available either to the medium or to their departed namesakes when alive. Broad was writing, too, before Soal's "Gordon Davis" and "John Ferguson" cases.

This brings us at least to the point where something can be said about the future. With appropriate reserve, four points may be made: *First*, it seems that the possibilities of what, rather unfairly, might be called the "purely observational" study of the psychology of mediums and their trance personalities have been at least temporarily pretty well exhausted. This is not to say that there is not still considerable statistical work to be done on the recorded material, in establishing and analysing the percentages of veridicality, for instance, on the lines of Saltmarsh's work on the sittings of Mrs. Warren Elliott, and in applying newly perfected techniques of assessment. And it is worth while to go on accumulating more material against the day when developments elsewhere will throw fresh light on it. The future lies in using more dynamic techniques. Already we have stressed the desirability of following up Mr. Whately Carington's initiative by applying standard psychological tests. It might conceivably also be interesting if one or two mediums could be psychoanalysed.

Second, in spite of the unimpressive results achieved so far, it would be worth trying with improved technique and more extensively the method of test questions, especially as it demands little time or effort and promises big returns. The basic idea is that before they die people should settle on some item of information, known only to themselves, which they intend to try to communicate after death. The hope is that if this were achieved fairly often it would provide an almost knockdown proof of survival. It would be far harder—though not necessarily impossible—to produce an alternative account in terms of paranormal transactions among the living. The usual technique has been to deposit in a bank or with the S.P.R. a sealed envelope containing some object or message. This has two flaws: first, that even if the correct information was duly provided, this achievement could be attributed to clairvoyance by the medium; second, that once the seal is broken the experiment is finished, and so even if the depositor had actually survived, his plan might be frustrated by bogus attempts or by his own preliminary failures. Dr. R. H. Thouless has now suggested an improved technique. This is to deposit an enciphered message to which the depositor has to supply the key after he is dead. The correct key will reveal a meaning in the cipher passage, whereas bogus and abortive attempts will not wreck the test. This technique is quite simple. If others will follow Thouless's lead, those who survive (in the ordinary way) can but await the results (see *Proc. S.P.R.*, Vol. XLVIII, pp. 253 ff. *and* pp. 342 ff.). Or rather, this is not strictly accurate: they can positively assist by providing a control. For Thouless's future communications, if such we are to have, would be the more impressive if efforts were made to extract the key in his lifetime using the supposed paranormal faculties (ESP) of mediums: but failed. Irreverence in this connection is perhaps justified by the failures of previous Communicators to pass such tests. "Sir Oliver Lodge," for instance, has failed to pass tests arranged by Sir Oliver Lodge.

Third, although we have been able to point to non-spiritualistic parallels to the main phenomena of spirit mediumship, it must be admitted that the available material is neither so abundant nor always so well-authenticated as one might wish. This gap should if possible be filled. Of course attempts might be abortive. But if so this very fact would obviously be significant, and might perhaps make strongly against a telepathic account. The reasons why this has not been done before seem to be, partly that there are certain peculiar difficulties involved, and partly that nearly all investigators—irrespective of their views and preferences about survival—have been under the spell of the spiritualist model of the situation. The difficulties arise from the fact that it is precisely in those countries where psychical research is strongest that Spiritualism is most influential. It is in these countries that the gifts and tendencies which are required to make a medium are most likely to develop, and set, into the accepted spiritualist pattern. So the most experienced workers are unlikely to be able to find and investigate people whose gifts developed into a different pattern. And with orthodox mediums there are serious ethical and practical restrictions on investigation. A sincere medium, believing she has a special gift and mission to console the bereaved, cannot be expected to co-operate with people who try to raise bogus spirits or otherwise to misuse the machinery of "communication". Hence the S.P.R. has developed a strict code of investigation. Dr. Soal's experiences with the bogus "John Ferguson" and "Gordon Davis" came as spontaneous uncovenanted blessings. Yet, even allowing for the difficulties, and even within this strict and proper code, more might well have been done but for the almost universal fascination of a spiritualist model. More would be done if that spell could be broken. This is a chicken-and-egg problem. It is not that all the people who have worked in this branch have come to spiritualist conclusions. They have not. It is rather that they seem nearly all to have been so gripped by the séance set-up, and so enthralled by the enormous—not necessarily or to everyone attractive—possibility of survival, that whatever answers they have given their questions have nearly always been spiritualist questions.

Fourth, one of the best hopes of advance here (as elsewhere in psychical research) lies in the experimental ESP work. The hope is that this may reveal what favours, what inhibits, and what are the limits of ESP capacity (i.e. telepathy and clairvoyance, whether retrocognitive,

precognitive, or simultaneous). And consequently that the
experimentally acquired knowledge will steadily provide
justification (or perhaps not) of our preference (which is,
we have argued, entirely warranted by the facts available
now) for an ESP, rather than for any spiritist, interpretation. Certainly we shall never understand what goes on in
séances till we know far more about ESP. This is one more
reason for the general shift of interest towards experiment
and statistics in the last twenty years.

Before passing to this there is a deeper level of
criticism of survivalism. The gist is that it is not clear
what such a theory will mean. Logically this question
should be prior to those raised so far. But it is so surprising as to justify a roundabout approach. For surely
Butler is right? Can we not understand the hopes of the
warriors of Allah who expect if they die in Holy War to go
straight to the arms of the black-eyed houris in Paradise?
Can we not understand the fears of the slum mother kept
from the contraceptive clinic by her priest's warnings of
penalties for those who die in mortal sin? Or even the
hopes of a Myers or a Sidgwick? Of course we can. It
would be a preposterous piece of over-sophistication to
fail to understand such fears and hopes, and to discount
their possible power and influence.[5]

But still the sceptic urges: surely something crucial
is being overlooked? For this future life is supposed to
continue even after physical dissolution: even after the
slow corruption in the cemetery, or the swift consumption
in the crematorium. To suggest that we might survive this
dissolution seems like suggesting that a nation might out-
last the annihilation of all its members. Certainly we can
understand the promises of Paradise, the threats of Hell,
the brave stories of Valhalla. But to expect that after my
death and dissolution such things might happen to me is to
overlook that by the hypothesis I shall not then exist. To
expect such things, through overlooking this, is surely
like accepting a fairy tale as history, through ignoring
the prefatory rubric "once upon a time, in a world that
never was . . . ?"

Of course the insinuations of the sceptic are as slick
and crude as they are unfair. But they can serve to throw

---

[5]Those who issued in the 1948 Italian election the monitory
poster with "Stalin cannot see you: but God can" printed
over a picture of a polling-booth, made no such mistake.
To say nothing of Plato (*Republic*, I and X) and Aristotle
(*Metaphysics* 1074B).

into relief two easily and often neglected but crucial
points. First, that the essence of doctrines of personal
survival (or immortality)—and this alone is what gives
them their huge human interest—is that they should assert
that we shall exist after our deaths (for ever). It is
thus, and only thus, that they can provide the basis for
expecting that we shall have "experiences" after death,
that with death things for us will not cease, but change.
For nothing can happen to us then unless there is still
an us for it to happen to. Second, that person-words
mean what they do mean. Words such as "you," "I," "person," "people," "woman," "man," "Flew"—though very different in their particular functions—are all used to refer
in one way or another to objects (the pejorative flavour of
this word should here be discounted) which you can point at,
touch, hear, see, and talk to. Person-words refer to people. And how can such objects as people survive physical
dissolution? This is a massive difficulty, and the need to
evade or remove it has provided the conscious or unconscious driving force for many intellectual manœuvres:

First, there have been attempts to show that person-
words have at most a contingent, and not a necessary reference to objects: that is to say that people as a matter of
fact (which might have been, and may one day be otherwise)
inhabit, or are otherwise closely associated with, their
bodies; but that the reference to objects is no part of the
meaning of person-words. These attempts have usually appeared as arguments that people are—inexplicably—com-
pounded of two elements, body and soul, the latter sufficiently elusive and insubstantial to be a plausible candi-
date for survival after dissolution; and that the soul is
the—real or essential—person. This last equation is crucial. Unless I am my soul, the immortality (or survival)
of my soul will not be my immortality, and the news of the
immortality (or future survival) of my soul would be of no
more concern to me than the news that my appendix would be
preserved eternally in a bottle. In psychical research
contexts the term "spirit" has usually done duty for the
less secular "soul."

Second, it has been thought that a doctrine of "the
resurrection of the body" (better perhaps reformulated as
"the reconstitution of the person") avoids this difficulty.
In spiritualist contexts this move has taken the form of
the view that people have (or are) "spiritual" or "astral"
bodies (or persons) which (or who) at death detach themselves from their "physical" or "earth-plane" bodies. But
this is surely to jump from the frying-pan of logical difficulty into the fire of factual indefensibility.

Third, whether or not talk of people surviving dissolution is, according to current usage, self-contradictory
(whether or not person-words refer to objects which could
not significantly be said to survive physical dissolution),
it has been argued that we can attach sense to talk of spirits surviving physical dissolution. We can. But the difficulty is to attach a sense such that this talk will, if
true, justify us in nourishing expectations of experiences,
instead of oblivion, after our deaths. It is in their
present use with its essential reference to certain objects
one can point at (viz. people) that person-words carry
their crucial implications. It is in this present use that
personal identity is the necessary condition of both ac-
countability and expectation. Which is only to say that it
is unjust to reward or punish someone for something unless
as a minimum condition he is the same person as did the
deed; and also that it is absurd to expect experiences for
Flew in 1984 unless in that year there is going to be someone who will be the same person as I. The problem is to
change the meaning of person-words so radically that it
becomes significant to talk of people surviving dissolution,
without changing it to such an extent that the crucial implications would be lost; and without losing touch with the
facts as far as we know them. The problem is to give a
sense to "Flew disembodied" or "the spirit of Flew" such
that the spirit of Flew will still be the same person as
the writer of this book, and such too that there will still
be some point in talking like this in a psychical research
context.

This is not a clearly hopeless task. But it certainly
is far harder than, and partly of a different kind from,
what is often thought. It is not clearly hopeless because
people though objects are objects of a very remarkable kind:
people unlike things have "private experiences"—feelings,
sensations, and so forth. And particular people have a
large range of, so to speak, separable characteristics—
knowledge of this and that, such-and-such peculiar mannerisms, and so on. And while people—the objects we can
point at—cannot conceivably survive physical dissolution,
private experiences might perhaps be significantly said to
occur disembodied. And some of the characteristics we have
been accustomed to associate with particular people could
conceivably be, and in fact sometimes actually are, mani-
fested in the absence of those people—those objects we
could once have pointed at. These two peculiarities of
people as objects suggest that the task is not hopeless.

But it is far harder than it might seem. For our language—and this of course applies just as much to person-

words and all the other words we use in our discourse about persons, as to the words for material things—has been evolved as an instrument for dealing with the situations in which men have found themselves: for the situations of this world. When we try—as we are trying when we want to speak of people surviving death—to use it for dealing with radically different conditions it breaks down. It begins to play tricks on us in all sorts of subtle and unexpected ways. For so many words which one might think to transfer easily to descriptions of putative spirit beings involve covert but essential reference to the corporeal. This fact is concealed from us by (and is doubtless also partly the cause of) our tendency tacitly, or even explicitly, to take spirit existence to be some sort of desubstantialized replica of the world we live in. Spirit cigars and astral trousers have often been derided. It is almost impossible to realize that our supposed bodiless beings really would be bodiless, and all that this involves. My feelings are distinguished from yours by being, as it were, attached to me and not to you. But disembodied experiences could not be "grouped" and "owned" in the same way at all. And it is no use relying on the fact that any person knows very well when he has a feeling that it is his. Because the whole question at issue is precisely this, whether any sense can be given to talk of disembodied people, and of their having feelings and so on.

The problem of creating suitable senses for "person" and associated terms and expressions would also be partly of an unexpected kind. For if the existence of disembodied people in the sense to be specified is to be a doctrine of survival, is to justify living people ("people" in the old sense) in expecting experiences after death, then it will have to make sense to talk of a disembodied person (new or extended sense of "person") being the same person as some former person (ordinary sense of "person"). And this will demand a change in the meaning of "same person". A disembodied person, a spirit, cannot be the same person as an (ordinary) person, in the present sense of "same person". For, to speak very dogmatically, the meaning and the criteria of this expression involve reference to the continuance of a particular object, the person in question. In the nature of the case this cannot apply to the case of a disembodied spirit. We shall have both to produce a sense of "same person" which could do the trick, and to provide a convincing quasi-legal argument for thus changing the use of that expression.

This is a difficult business. Perhaps an analogy would make things clearer. Constantly courts are confronted with

perplexing issues which take the form of questions, but
which are not so much questions asking for answers as
demands requiring decision. "Is a flying-boat a ship?"
Well, of course, it is and yet it isn't. But the court has
to decide one way or the other. The problem arises because
an attempt is being made to use a word in a situation with
which it was never designed to cope. A law which was
passed before flying-boats were thought of has been contra-
vened (or has it?) by a flying-boat. "Is a flying-boat a
ship?" does not really ask for information about either
flying-boats or ships, nor yet even for linguistic information about the present and proper use of the words "flying-
boat" and "ship". It demands a decision as to what the
future proper legal use is to be; whether or not the term
"ship" is to cover flying-boats. It would be naïve either
to wonder whether a flying-boat is really a ship (whatever
that might mean) or to be taken in by the legal fiction
that the Legislature—working before flying-boats were
thought of—either did or did not intend to include them
when it used the word "ships." Now, person-words and their
associates were developed to deal with the activities and
transactions of the objects we call people. If we want to
stretch them to describe the supposed activities and transactions of putative incorporeal beings, then we must not be
surprised if we find things going wrong, if we discover
that what used to be straight questions now turn out sometimes to be crooked. "Is this (spirit the same person as)
Myers?" is not susceptible of a straight-forward yes-or-no
answer; though we could make a decision (and a reasoned decision such as the lawyers make) about the use of "same
person," in terms of which a definite answer might then be
given. The question "Is this (spirit the same person as)
Myers?" is very much more like the question "Is it chess if
you play without the king?"[6] than it is like "Is it Soal
who keeps ringing me up?"

Professor H. H. Price has tried to give a suitable
sense to "disembodied survival" in a fascinating explora-
tion (*Proc. S.P.R.*, Vol L, pp. 1 ff.).[7] With great skill
he indicates a conceivable mode of existence of possible
conscious but incorporeal beings. The crux is that such
beings might have a life of mental imagery, and little else.
This suggestion seems to make sense, even if the occurrence
of mental imagery without a "physical basis" in a brain is—

---

[6]Wittgenstein's example was, I believe, significantly different: "Is it chess if you play without the queen?"

[7][See pp. 21-47 above—Ed.]

as, apart possibly from the facts of psychical research, we
have every reason to suppose—as a matter of fact impossible. For it would always be significant, though often silly, in the fact of no matter what behavioural[8] evidence to
the contrary, to suggest that someone might or might not be
in pain or might or might not be having a mental image.
There would be no contradiction in asserting the behavioural evidence and denying its usual experiential correlate.
Consider the nightmare case, borrowed from Professor John
Wisdom, of the man who says to a patient being wheeled into
the operating theatre: "You'll make no sound, no movement,
and afterwards you will remember nothing: but, in spite of
the anæsthetic, you'll feel it all." Or consider the reports of people after cataleptic trances saying that their
experience was continuous, though they had appeared oblivi-
ous, which provoked Edgar Allan Poe's tormented tales of
burial alive.

Now Price's account of his image beings avoids the
cruder errors of purporting to describe disembodied existence while surreptitiously reintroducing bodies. This is
no mean achievement. For even Plato when speaking supposed-
ly of the life of incorporeal souls disembodied by death
describes their fortunes in precisely the terms of a (corporeal) adventure; as when he sees [*sic*] souls under physical
tortures, which only corporeal people could suffer (see *Republic*, X). But Price still assumes that simply by providing this account he has shown that conceivably we might
become such beings after death, that death for us might be
a metamorphosis from a substantial to an insubstantial mode
of existence. On the contrary—as we have argued—it is
still necessary to show that it would be reasonable, if
certain conditions were satisfied, to decide that particular incorporeal beings could be identified with, could be
said to be the same persons as, particular human beings.
The word "decide" is crucial. The present meanings of our
person-words and expressions are adapted to the needs and
facts of this world. We cannot extend them to cover the
radically different possibilities of another world without,

---

[8]The word "behavioural" is being used to cover not merely
what he *does*, but also—what is so often and so importantly
contrasted with this—what he *says*. It is the failure both
of psychologists and laymen to notice how crucially different this is from the ordinary sense (which covers the former only) which has been partly but only partly responsible
for the scandal of behaviourism. Here, for good measure,
we also intend the word to cover neurological occurrences.

tacitly or explicitly, deciding to make drastic alterations in their use, their meanings. This may sound a tortuous method of remaking a trivial point. But the point only sounds trivial in the context of a speculative discussion, where it is always open to us so to arrange our suppositions about possible beings that it would be obviously reasonable to extend our notions of person and personal identity to include these. But the facts of any actual other world may be such that we should not want to decide, even in the light of the fullest knowledge, that a particular insubstantial being either was or was not Myers. Price, by speaking about what it might be like for us to be incorporeal beings takes these vital decisions for granted.

He seems momentarily to have overlooked that in questions about personal identity even the honest testimony of that person does not necessarily provide the last word, as it does where the issue is whether or not someone is in pain. He writes, "And surely the important question is what constitutes my personal identity *for myself*" (p. 31). But Capone either is or is not the one who led the gang. He cannot be one thing for himself and another for other people; though some (usually but not always including himself; memory is not infallible) may be in the secret, while others are not. It is because this is so, because it is possible to be mistaken as to whether one did or suffered something, whereas it makes no sense to talk of being *mistaken* as to whether one is now in pain, that one cannot get around these points about *decision* issues by, as it were, appealing to a possible incorporeal being "himself" (or itself) to settle expertly whether or not "he" (or it) is Myers.[9] Unless, of course, one is prepared to abdicate the decision itself to the "spirits": which is itself a decision; and a very poor one.

---

[9]To bring out this difficult point, consider two fantastic examples: suppose a person P split like an amoeba into two identical people P_1 and P_2 *both* claiming to be P and both having the "memories" appropriate to and all other characteristics of the original person before his great divide: and suppose two incorporeal beings *both* claimed to be Myers, and *both* displayed the appropriate characteristics and "memories." Here testimony, albeit honest, could not be the last word: unless we are willing to say that in this case two things which are the same as a third can be different from one another; as we might indeed *decide* to do. (See my "Locke and the Problem of Personal Identity," *Philosophy* 1951.)

The argument of this chapter has been of two quite different, but interrelated, kinds: first about the possible interpretations of facts, and then about the meanings of words. *First*, we indicated the lines on which apparently strong evidence for survival might be interpreted more simply in terms of telepathy etc. among living people only. This is a type of argument long familiar, at least to psychical researchers. *Second*, we tried to show that there are serious difficulties involved in giving sense to talk of spirits and their survival. This line of argument is not yet nearly so familiar, even to those who devote themselves to this subject. The crux is not that our possible future life would be so different from anything we know that we cannot hope to describe or imagine it. The crux is that these spirits, if we gave determinate meaning to this term, might, precisely because of their incorporeality, be so different from what we now mean by "people" that we could not identify them with people who had once lived, even though they might possess peculiar knowledge and other characteristics reminiscent of our dead friends.

Part Four Religious Belief
and the Afterlife

TOWARDS A CHRISTIAN THEOLOGY OF DEATH

John Hick

In order that we may start from where we are, and may be reminded of where this is by contrast with somewhere else, let me begin by reading to you two passages from the world we have lost—the world in which the belief in a life to come was a pervasive factor in most people's minds, affecting their attitudes both to life and to death.   The first passage comes from a book of legal precedents published in London in 1592, when the first Elizabeth was on the throne of England and when Will Shakespeare was a rising London playwright.   The book offers "a verie perfect form of a Will", which begins as follows:

In the name of God, Amen.   The twenty-sixth day of April in the year of our Lord God, one thousand five hundred and ninety two, A.B.C. the unprofitable servant of God, weak in body, but strong in mind, do willingly and with a free heart render and give again into the hands of my Lord God and Creator, my spirit, which he of his fatherly goodness gave unto me, when he first fashioned me in my mother's womb, making me a living creature, nothing doubting that for his infinite mercies, set forth in the precious blood of his dearly beloved son Jesus Christ our alone saviour and redeemer, he will receive my soul into his glory, and place it in the company of the heavenly angels and blessed saints.   And as concerning my body even with a good will and free heart I give over, commending it to the earth whereof it came, nothing doubting but according

This paper, originally read at a conference on *The Last Enemy* held at the University of Birmingham in March 1968, was first printed in *Dying, Death, and Disposal*, edited by Gilbert Cope, published by the Society for Promoting Christian Knowledge, London, 1970.   It is reprinted here with the permission of the author and publisher.

> to the article of my faith, at the great day of
> general resurrection when we shall all appear
> before the judgment seat of Christ, I shall re-
> ceive the same again by the mighty power of God,
> wherewith he is able to subdue all things to
> himself, not a corruptible, mortal, weak and
> vile body, as it is now, but an uncorruptible,
> immortal, strong, and perfect body in all points
> like unto the glorious body of my Lord and Sav-
> iour Jesus Christ . . .

and then the testator proceeds to the disposition of his
property.

Now this is of course a consciously correct form of
words according to the ideas of the time, offered as a
paradigm for the framing of wills; and we may perhaps be
tempted to wonder if it is more correct than sincere. But
I think that any such suspicion would be uncalled for.
These words reflect the real beliefs of real people.

As indirect evidence of this I cite a second passage.
This was written nearly 200 years later, and is to be found
in Boswell's *Life of Johnson*, where he transcribes a page
of Johnson's diary for Sunday, 18 October 1767.

> Yesterday, Oct. 17, at about ten in the morning,
> I took my leave for ever of my dear old friend,
> Catherine Chambers, who came to live with my
> mother about 1724, and has been but little parted
> from us since. She is now fifty-eight years old.
>
> I desired all to withdraw, then told her
> that we were to part for ever; that as Christians,
> we should part with prayer; and that I would, if
> she was willing, say a short prayer beside her.
> She expressed great desire to hear me; and held
> up her poor hands, as she lay in bed, with great
> fervour, while I prayed, kneeling by her, nearly
> in the following words:
>
> "Almighty and most merciful Father, whose
> loving kindness is over all thy works, behold,
> visit, and relieve this thy servant, who is
> grieved with sickness. Grant that the sense of
> her weakness may add strength to her faith, and
> seriousness to her repentance. And grant that by
> the help of thy Holy Spirit, after the pains and
> labours of this short life, we may all obtain
> everlasting happiness, through Jesus Christ our
> Lord; for whose sake hear our prayers. Amen."
>
> I then kissed her. She told me, that to
> part was the greatest pain she had ever felt, and

that she hoped we should meet again in a better
place. I expressed, with swelled eyes, and great
emotion of tenderness the same hopes. We kissed,
and parted. I humbly hope to meet again, and to
part no more.

Here there is I think no mistaking the genuine and full sin-
cerity of the beliefs that are expressed.

These documents, with their presuppositions, come as I
have said (using Peter Laslett's recent title), from the
world we have lost. The firm assumption that this life is
part of a much larger existence which transcends our earthly span is no longer a part of the thought world of today.
Post-Christian secular man believes only in what he experiences, plus that which the accredited sciences reveal to
him. The afterlife falls outside this sphere and is accordingly dismissed as a fantasy of wishful thinking. Of
course not everyone you meet in the streets is an example
of post-Christian secular man come of age, as depicted after Bonhoeffer. On the contrary, many different phases of
pre-Christian, Christian, and post-Christian existence co-
exist in our culture and even sometimes within the same
individual. There may even in our society as a whole be
more pre-Christianity than post-Christianity, with more
people believing in astrology than astronomy, or putting
their faith in horoscopes rather than in microscopes as
means to knowledge. So far as afterlife beliefs are concerned, a B.B.C. report of 1955 suggested that about 43%
of its public (which is virtually coterminous with the pop-
ulation as a whole) believes in a life after death. If
such is the nation-wide state of mind on the subject, there
is good evidence that this has influenced opinion within
the churches, drawing it down towards this half-hearted (or
to be more precise 43%-hearted) level of belief. For example the Mass Observation document *Puzzled People*, published
in 1948, reported that "Of those who say they believe in a
Deity, one in five are definite in their assertion that
they do not believe in a life after death." And in the Gal-
lup Poll's *Television and Religion* survey, published in
1964, it emerged that some 74% of Roman Catholics in this
country believe in an afterlife, some 56% of Free Churchmen, and some 49% of Anglicans. These figures are for the
official or nominal memberships. The figures for regular
church attenders are higher and are grouped closer together,
namely Roman Catholics 88%, Free Churchmen 86%, and Anglicans 85%. But that there are 12-15% of regular committed
worshippers who do not believe in a life after death is
surely significant, and indicates a fairly marked movement
away from traditional Christian teaching on the matter.

And this negative attitude, which may for some 15% of
church members be simply an assumption absorbed from the
surrounding culture, has been turned by some of our more
radical theologians into a principle for the reinterpreta-
tion of Christianity. Authentic Christianity, they say,
has no place for afterlife beliefs. Christians are not and
ought not to be interested in the possibility of an existence after death. We ought instead to be wholly interested
in this world and in our contemporary neighbours, with
their and our pressing human needs and problems.

In commenting upon this point of view may I begin by
indicating my personal starting point?

In general I have far more sympathy with the new theologians than with the old theologians. I regard the contemporary breaking of long-established religious thought
forms as good, and as having inaugurated a period in which
there are exciting possibilities of reconstruction and chal-
lenging scope for originality. Thus in face of the contemporary theological ferment I do not, when I try to look into my own mind, feel reactionary, censorious, or defensive.
I have even, when I was in the United States, been involved
in a heresy case, when a very conservative minority sought
to exclude me from the ministry of the United Presbyterian
Church for declining to affirm one of the more manifestly
mythological aspects of the Christian tradition. I mention
this simply to indicate that if I now proceed to criticize
the understanding of death offered by the new theology this
criticism does not necessarily come out of a generally reactionary attitude, nor out of a constitutional failure to
comprehend or sympathize with the new. But I am nevertheless bothered by a tendency in popular radical theology today to set up false, because over-simple, alternatives, and
consequently to arrive at unwarranted conclusions.

It appears to me that in this matter of the afterlife
we have a case in point. On the one hand, it seems obviously true that we should not so set our thoughts upon a life
to come as to undervalue or fail to engage unreservedly
with this present earthly existence. Christianity is concerned with the transformation of human life here and now.
Salvation is not something to be postponed to another
sphere beyond the grave; eternal life (whatever else it may
be) is a quality of living to be entered into now. All
this is surely both true and enormously important. But it
does not follow or even begin to follow, that there is no
life after death. I shall suggest a little later how the
two themes of immortality and this-worldliness are fully
compatible with one another. But I would simply point out
at the moment that the fact that we ought not, in the midst

of this life, to distract ourselves by dwelling upon a life
to come, does not entail that this earthly existence, upon
which we are now meant to be concentrating, is all.   The
question of a life after death must be decided in some other way.

Unless, then, we choose to regard ourselves as simply
the priests of human culture, affirming—only more so—what
our culture affirms and denying what it denies, the fact
that the public mind of our day is tending away from belief
in a life after death does not settle the matter.   There remains the possibility that Christianity is committed by its
sources and its nature to the claim that the structure of
reality is other than that which our contemporary culture
as a whole believes it to be.   And so we have to raise directly the question whether the belief in an afterlife is
or is not an essential part of the Christian faith.   Upon
this issue every other aspect of our theology of death necessarily hinges.

There are two broad divergent alternatives for Christian thought in relation to each of its main traditional
tenets, including eschatology (i.e. its discourse concerning "the last things", one of which is death).   In philosophical terms, one of these alternatives is realist and
the other reductionist.   To outline the latter first: it
claims that the meaning of the various Christian doctrines
can be wholly stated in terms of present human experience
and involves no claim that goes beyond this.   The meaning,
for example, of the doctrine of creation is that we accept
the world as basically good; the doctrine expresses (I
quote Paul van Buren) "an affirmative view of the world of
men and things".[1]   Again, the meaning of the doctrine of
the divinity of Christ is that we take him as our Lord.
And in the same pattern the meaning of the doctrine of
eternal life is our affirmation that the life of faith has
unlimited value and significance.   There is thus in each
case a reduction of—to use a variety of terms—the metaphysical to the psychological, or the ontological to the
existential, or the transcendent to the immanent.   In contrast to this, theological realism affirms both dimensions
and refuses to reduce the one to the other.   It does not of
course deny that it is part of the meaning of creation that
the world is good; or that it is part of the meaning of the
divinity of Christ that he is our Lord; or that it is part
of the meaning of eternal life that the life of faith has
unlimited worth.   It is not concerned to say less than this

---

[1]*The Secular Meaning of the Gospel*, p. 177.

but in each case to say more than this. And so far as
eternal life is concerned it claims not only that the life
in relation to God has unlimited value but also that this
value is embodied in unlimited existence. The ultimately
valuable is also the ultimately real. That which God affirms is held in being by his creative love; and accordingly eternal life is also the life everlasting.

There are two main grounds on which this may be af-
firmed. One is that the teaching of Jesus is so pervaded
by the belief in a life after death that it is hardly possible to base one's religious faith upon him, as the revelation of God's love to man, and yet to reject so integral a
part of his conception of the divine purpose. I don't
think that I need cite a series of New Testament passages
to establish that Jesus believed in a future life. I will
only mention, by way of reminder, the parables of Dives and
Lazarus and of the sheep and the goats; the controversy
with the Sadducees about the general resurrection; and the
numerous sayings about future judgement. I have in fact
never heard of a New Testament scholar who denied that Jesus believed in an afterlife; and the point can probably
safely be taken as non-controversial.

If we now go on to ask *why* Jesus believed so firmly
in an afterlife, the answer points to the second possible
ground for this faith, namely, that it is a corollary of
belief in the sovereign heavenly Father. For there would
be an intolerable contradiction in affirming on the one
hand that God knows, values, and loves each of his human
creatures as unique individuals, and invokes in them the
desire to realize the highest potentialities of their nature in response to his claim upon them, and yet on the
other hand that he has ordained their extinction when they
have only just begun to fulfil the divine purpose which has
endowed them with those potentialities and aspirations.
The divine love and the divine demand alike bestow upon man
a dignity transcending that of the beasts that perish. As
Martin Luther said, "Anyone with whom God speaks, whether
in wrath or in mercy, the same is certainly immortal. The
Person of God who speaks, and the Word, show that we are
creatures with whom God wills to speak, right into eternity,
and in an immortal manner."[2]

Luther is of course here making the large assumption
that eternal life must mean, or at least must include in
its meaning, the continued existence of distinct individual
human personalities after their bodily death. But—let us

---

[2]Quoted by Emil Brunner, *Dogmatics*, II, 69.

now ask—is not this a rather crassly literal idea, the
sort of thing that today we almost automatically demytholo-
gize? May we not think instead, for example, of some kind
of merging of consciousnesses in a larger whole, a losing
of individual personality in something more inclusive, a
fulfilment of human existence which does not involve the
perpetuation of separate strands of consciousness? Here
one time-honoured picture is that of the drop returning to
the ocean from which it was temporally separated.

Needless to say, we *can* think in such terms as these;
but the question is whether they will satisfy the exigen-
cies of Christian faith which led us to speak of eternal
life in the first place. If we affirm the life to come because of Jesus' teaching, it seems that we shall find ourselves affirming continued individual personal existence.
If we affirm it as a corollary of the love of God for his
human children, again it would seem that we shall be affirming the continuance of the individual personality. It is
indeed hard to see on what specifically Christian ground
one would affirm human immortality and yet not affirm it as
involving continued personal identity.

But if a conception of eternal life in which human personality is explicitly denied a place fails to satisfy the
two interlocking motives of Christian eschatology, may we
not fall back upon complete agnosticism concerning the form
of the life to come and simply declare that in some unimag-
inable way God's good purpose for mankind will be fulfilled?
Death does not cancel God's love for us; and we must rest
in this faith without attempting to picture its implications in quasi-earthly terms. Whether it involves continued separate individuality we do not know and we ought not
to care. Sufficient that, whatever its nature, our destiny
will be determined by the goodness of God. Such a modest
and undogmatic approach can hardly fail to appeal to all of
us. And yet I think we can also see that it stands in real
danger of meaninglessness. Is it a responsible use of language to speak of eternal life, immortality, the life to
come, heaven and hell, and then to add that this language
carries no implications whatever regarding the continuation
or otherwise of human personality beyond the grave? Are we
not evacuating our words of all meaning—whilst however retaining their comforting emotive overtones—if we speak at
the grave side of the "sure and certain hope of resurrection to eternal life" and yet add as theologians that this
hope is completely neutral as between the deceased's present and future existence and non-existence?

I must confess that this seems to me to come perilous-
ly close to double-talk. And yet this kind of language is

often heard. Let us consider an actual example, which is
to be found in the chapter on "Life after death" in Bishop
John Robinson's recent popular book *But That I can't Believe!* (1967). This is a book to which on the whole I respond sympathetically. It seems to me a bold and on the
whole a successful attempt to communicate the Christian
faith in the language of the *Sunday Mirror*, and this is
both a difficult and an important thing to do. But the
subject of death and resurrection inevitably stands out as
an embarrassment for the "new theologian"; for it confronts
him with an unmistakable form of the issue which his whole
theology is designed to de-emphasize, the issue of transcendence. On the one hand he does not want absolutely and
definitively to deny transcendence, for he is aware that
ultimately only this can give religious substance to his
faith. But on the other hand, knowing that contemporary
post-Christian secular man has no use for the idea of the
transcendent, he does not want to rely upon it in communicating the gospel. He finds himself wanting both to affirm it and not to affirm it; hence the air of double-talk
that is so liable to pervade his discussion. To turn to
our example, we find Robinson saying that in the New Testament eternal life is not a doctrine of survival after bodily death but of "a quality of life—here and now—which
death cannot touch. Death is put in its place, as power-
less to make any difference" (p. 45). This, he notes,
agrees with the contemporary attitude that "Death may be
the end. So what?" (p. 45). Accordingly, Robinson concludes that "nothing turns on what happens after death"
(p. 46). He is apparently saying in this aspect of his discussion that eternal life is a quality of existence available to mankind now, and that to affirm it as the gift of
Christ is compatible with the contemporary secular assumption that death means personal extinction. But then, talking in a different vein, Robinson also says (p. 46):

> As a Christian, I know my life to be grounded in
> a love which will not let me go. It comes to me
> as something completely unconditional. If it
> could really be put an end to by a bus on the way
> home it would not have the quality I know it to
> have. From such a love neither cancer nor the H-
> bomb can separate. Death cannot have the last
> word. . . . As St Paul says, "If in this life
> only we have hoped in Christ, we are of all men
> the most foolish."

Here, if words have any stable meaning, he is saying that
eternal life is a relationship to God which is not terminated by bodily death. And, if it is not terminated by
bodily death, then presumably it goes on after bodily death.
Surely, then, the secular reader will rightly want to know
whether Robinson is affirming a life after death or not;
and in either case he will want to have the matter stated
unambiguously and its consequences explicitly acknowledged.
(It is worth adding that this criticism does not apply to
Robinson's main book on this subject, *In the End, God* . . .).

It is I think to be noted that the logical relationship between the two views which are found side by side in
Robinson's chapter is an asymmetrical relationship. The
first excludes the second, but the second does not exclude
the positive part of the first. We do not have to choose
between the alternatives of eternal life as a present quality of existence and eternal life as immortal existence;
still less between an infinitely valuable quality with a
brief duration and a relatively valueless quality with unlimited duration. These are not the only possibilities.
The more authentically Christian view of the matter, I
would suggest, goes beyond this false alternative to the
conception of eternal life as unlimited both in value and
in duration, the link between the two being forged by the
love of God which unqualifiedly affirms and supports this
special quality of creaturely existence.

This is perhaps the point at which to identify a red
herring which sometimes misleads thought on these matters.
It is said—correctly—that the distinctively Christian doctrine is not one of immortality but of resurrection. So
far from being naturally immortal, as Plato for example
taught, the Bible teaches that man is made out of the dust
of the earth and is destined to be dissolved again into
that dust. But God by his own will and sovereign power recreates us after death in another sphere of being, bestow-
ing upon us a new life which is not a natural immortality
but a free gift of the Creator. From this starting point,
which represents in capsule the biblical view, some have
inferred that there is no Christian doctrine of immortality
and/or of human survival after death. But this does not
follow at all. The doctrine of God's resurrecting of the
dead is not the opposite of a doctrine of human immortality,
but is a form of that doctrine—namely, one in which man's
immortality is seen as a divine gift and as dependent upon
the will of God. This is quite clearly a doctrine of human
survival of bodily death and in that sense of man's immortality.

However, if Christianity is indeed committed to belief
in personal survival after death, both by its starting
point in the life and teaching of Jesus and by the logic of
its faith in the love of God for the finite beings made in
his image, there now opens before us a further set of op-
tions. For there are two major alternative theological
frameworks within which the Christian belief in an afterlife has developed; and these tend to produce two rather
different attitudes to death.

The tradition which has for the most part dominated
the Western Christian mind until our own time is based upon
the great imaginative picture, or myth, of the drama of salvation beginning with the fall of man and ending in the
division of humanity into the saved and the damned, segre-
gated in heaven and hell. Man was originally created as a
finitely perfect creature, but wickedly misused his freedom to rebel against God; and it was this original sin
that, in Milton's words, "brought death into the world, and
all our woe". Death is thus a punishment for, or a divinely ordained consequence or fruit of, sin—a consequence
brought upon the whole race by the sin of our first fore-
father, Adam. St Paul wrote that "sin came into the world
through one man and death through sin, and so death spread
to all men".[3] But it was St Augustine in the fifth century
who, elaborating Paul's thought in his own way, definitively projected the picture that has informed the Christian
imagination for 1,500 years. In the *City of God* he said
that "the first men were so created, that if they had not
sinned, they would not have experienced any kind of death;
but that, having become sinners, they were so punished with
death, that whatsoever sprang from their stock should also
be punished with the same death".[4]

On this view our mortality is not an aspect of the
divinely intended human situation, but is an evil, a state
that ought never to have come about, a disastrous consequence of man's turning away from his Maker. Death is a
punishment, and the emotions that appropriately reverberate
around it are those of guilt and sorrow, remorse and fear.

But the Christian mind has never adhered consistently
and exclusively to this understanding of mortality and to
the attitude which it renders appropriate. In addition to
this dark, punitive conception of the meaning of death
there has always been the very different picture of human
life as a pilgrimage, with bodily death as the end of one

---

[3]Rom. 5. 12.

[4]Book 13, chap. 3.

stage of that pilgrimage and, by the same token, as a passing on to another stage. This picture has in it a glint of gold, a note of fulfilment, of triumph, even of adventure in face of death, a note which is perfectly caught in John Bunyan's passage about the passing of that great pilgrim, Mr. Valiant-for-truth:

> After this it was noised abroad that Mr. Valiant-
> for-truth was taken with a summons by the same
> post as the other, and had this for a token that
> the summons was true, that his pitcher was bro-
> ken at the fountain. When he understood it, he
> called for his friends, and told them of it.
> Then said he, I am going to my fathers, and tho'
> with great difficulty I am got hither, yet now
> I do not repent me of all the trouble I have been
> at to arrive where I am. My sword I give to him
> that shall succeed me in my pilgrimage, and my
> courage and skill to him that can get it. My
> marks and scars I carry with me, to be a witness
> for me that I have fought his battles who now
> will be my rewarder. When the day that he must
> go hence was come, many accompanied him to the
> riverside, into which as he went he said, Death,
> where is thy sting? And as he went down deeper
> he said, Grave, where is thy victory? So he
> passed over, and all the trumpets sounded for
> him on the other side.

This pilgrim attitude to death is only at home within a different theological framework from the official Augustinian understanding of our mortality as a divinely inflicted punishment for sin. This different framework is to be found within the history of Christian thinking, though for most of the time only as a minority report overshadowed by the dominant Augustinian tradition. The alternative goes back through strands of Eastern Christianity to the early Hellenistic Fathers, and has been developed more fully in the modern period since it reappeared in the work of the great nineteenth-century German Protestant thinker, Friedrich Schleiermacher. On this view man was not created in a finitely perfect state from which he then fell, but was initially brought into being as an immature creature who was only at the beginning of a long process of moral growth and development. Man did not fall disastrously from a better state into one of sin and guilt, with death as its punishment, but rather he is still in process of being created. Irenaeus, in the second century, provided a vocabu-

lary for this teleological conception when he distinguished
between the image (*imago*) and the likeness (*similitudo*) of
God in man. Man as he has emerged from the slow evolution
of the forms of life exists as a rational and personal creature in the image of God. But he is still only the raw material for a further stage of the creative process by which
this intelligent animal is being brought through his own
free responses to his environment to that perfection of his
nature which is his finite likeness to God.

From this point of view the wide gap, marked by the
doctrine of the fall, between man's actual state and the
state intended for him in God's purpose, is indeed a reality. But the ideal state, representing the fulfilment of
God's intention for man, is not a lost reality, forfeited
long ago in "the vast backward and abysm of time", but something lying before us as a state to be attained in the dis-
tant future. And our present mortal embodied earthly life
is not a penal condition, but a time of soul-making in
which we may freely respond to God's purpose and become, in
St Paul's phrases, "children of God" and "heirs of eternal
life". For such a theology the proper function of our
earthly existence, with its baffling mixture of good and
evil, is to be an environment in which moral choices and
spiritual responses are called for, and in which men and
women are being formed in relationship to one another within a common world.

This theology prompts an understanding of the meaning
of life as a divinely intended opportunity, given to us
both individually and as a race, to grow towards the reali-
zation of the potentialities of our own nature and so to
become fully human. Life is thus aptly imaged in terms of
the ancient picture of an arduous journey towards the life
of the Celestial City. This pilgrimage crosses the fron-
tier of death; for its final end is not attained in this
life, and therefore if it is to be attained at all there
must be a further life, or lives, beyond bodily death in
which God's purpose continues to hold us in being in environments related to that purpose.

Accordingly death does not have the absolute significance that it has in the Augustinian theology as the moment
when the individual's eternal destiny is irrevocably decided. In that tradition the soul as it is at the moment
of bodily death faces a definitive divine judgement and re-
ceives either the gracious gift of eternal life or the just
wages of eternal death. But this traditional picture has
to be criticized in the light of modern biological, psychological, and sociological knowledge. The conditions of a
person's life as these are determined by his biological

inheritance, and by the influence of the family and the wider social matrix upon his early development, are often such as to make it virtually impossible that God's purpose for the individual will be fulfilled in this life. It would thus be intolerably unjust for such a victim of adverse circumstances to be eternally penalized. From the Christian premise of the goodness and love of God we must accordingly infer continued human life beyond death leading eventually to the far-distant fulfilment of the purpose for which we exist.

Within such a theological framework the question has to be encountered, why is there any such thing as death? If we die only to live again beyond death, why should we die at all? What can be the function of death within the divine purpose, as this kind of theology conceives of it?

I think that some of the things that existentialist writers have said about death point in the direction of an answer by stressing the way in which our mortality determines the shape and character of our lives. This is, I think, an important insight, to which I shall return presently. But before coming to that there is another related suggestion to be considered. It is sometimes said that a man's death gives *meaning* to his life. This is in fact said in two senses, each of which is worth looking at.

First, there is a sense in which a man's death, by completing his life, makes it possible for others to see its meaning. For only when a life has been rounded off by death are we able to see it in its totality and so to characterize it as a whole. And to be able to characterize it as a whole as a good life, or bad, as happy or unhappy, heroic or banal, creative or wasted, and so on, might be equated with seeing its nature and quality, or discerning its meaning. This seems to be true enough; but so far it supplies only a relatively trivial sense in which death gives meaning to life. It applies the general truth that you can only see a process in its totality once it has been completed; from which tautology it follows that one can only see a man's life as a totality after he has died. But nevertheless a life may *have* a meaning—a value, a direction, a purpose—whilst it is still being lived, even though it is only at death that the accounts can finally be closed and audited. Bertrand Russell, for example, is now ninety-seven years old and has already left much more than an average life-span of activity and writing to be surveyed, evaluated, praised, criticized. We do not have to wait until he dies to be able to see in his life a remarkable living out of the rationalist spirit. We can see his relentless intellectual honesty; the narrowness of some of his

thinking as well as the extreme clarity of all of it; the
shape of his life as fulfilling Plato's ideal of the philosophic life, which begins by attending to mathematics and
logic and ends in engagement with the concrete human problems of ethics and politics. And so massive and consistent
has been the quality of his life over this long period that
nothing he might do or fail to do now would undo the meaning of the life he has already lived. We are thus reminded
that the tautology that we can see a life as a whole, and
see the meaning of that whole, only when the life has terminated, is in some cases merely trivial and unilluminating.

But there is a second sense in which a man's death may
give meaning to his life, namely that the manner of his dying may throw a flood of retrospective light upon his character throughout life. The analogy has been used of the
final resolving chord of a melody: only when this last
chord is heard does the melody as a whole emerge. The last
act, the act of dying, instead of being just one more event
in a man's biography, may constitute a peculiarly crucial
and illuminating climax. For example, one who had seemed
through lack of severe temptation to be a person of integrity may die ignominiously trying to save himself at the
expense of a number of others, and this selfish end then
colours our appreciation of his character and of his life
as a whole. Or on the other hand an apparently very ordinary man, living an inconspicuously decent and honest life,
may in some great crisis sacrifice his life to save others;
and then this death reveals to us a quality that was im-
plicit in his life as a whole. He was all that time a man
capable of heroic self-sacrifice, though until this last
crisis that quality showed itself only in the quiet integrity of his life. Now, however, there is a final burst of
illumination in the light of which that integrity takes on
a stronger and more dramatic colour.

In parenthesis let me say that by analogy this may
suggest a way of understanding the significance, for Christianity, of the death of Jesus. That is to say, Jesus'
death has special significance as revealing the significance of his life and work as a whole. His life was a
complex event in which the divine love towards mankind was
seen at work on earth in the midst of human history; and
the depth of that love was finally and definitively revealed by Jesus' willingness to be crucified rather than
deny the saving significance of his own life and teaching.
In contrast to the traditional satisfaction and penal-
substitutionary atonement theories this means that the significance of Christ's death did not reside in the event itself considered in isolation and as effective *ex opere*

operato. Christ's saving work was his ministry as a whole. But within this his passion and death have special significance as revealing the dominant motive and meaning of his life.

There is, then, a sense in which a death may give meaning to a life by illuminating the significance already inherent in it. But such illumination is somewhat exceptional. It occurs only in the case of a death, such as martyrdom, that is in some special way striking and significant. But most deaths are simply the chronological end of a life, and throw little or no additional light upon the meaning of that life. Or they may be the kind of death that is positively destructive of meaning because it breaks into a life prematurely and yet stands in no organic relation to that life and its quality. It is this that makes the atheistic existentialist Jean-Paul Sartre speak of "the absurd character of death".[5] He notes that death may at any moment violently strike a man down in mid-career by accident or disease, leaving his work unfinished, his relationships unfulfilled, his plans disrupted, his potentialities undeveloped. We are all of us, at least until old age, subject to this possibility. And for Sartre the fact that death as arbitrary destruction may befall anyone vitiates the meaning of life. "Thus," he says, "death is never that which gives life its meaning; it is, on the contrary, that which on principle removes all meaning from life."[6]

Sartre is surely exaggerating—and indeed does not a good deal of existentialist thought consist in precisely this kind of exaggeration?—when he says that the possibility of premature death renders all life meaningless and absurd. (Does for example the possibility that Bertrand Russell may be run over by a bus in his ninety-eighth year now render his already long life meaningless?) However, just as others have been right in saying that in some cases a man's death discloses the meaning of his life, so also Sartre is right in saying that in some cases death deprives a life of meaning. Death can have both this meaning-bestowing and this meaning-destroying effect. And what, as it seems to me, Christianity has to say at this point is that neither this meaning nor this meaninglessness is absolute and final. Death is the end of the chapter but not of the book; or better, it is the end of the volume but not of the whole work. This life has its own autonomy and may have its own

---

[5] *Being and Nothingness*, p. 533.

[6] Ibid., p. 539.

completeness; and all our present activities have to be related to it and to terminate within it. And yet, according
to Christianity, death is nevertheless not extinction. The
meaning developed in this life, in so far as it is good, is
to be taken forward into a larger pattern of larger value;
and the meaningless thread of a life without value is not
to be cut but is to be carried forward and eventually woven
into the same pattern of larger and indeed unlimited value.

And yet it remains a valid insight that it is the
boundaries that give to anything its shape; and there is an
important sense in which the boundary of death provides the
distinctive shape and character of our human life. Consider as an analogy the contribution which the regularly recur-
ring boundaries of sleep make to the nature of our human
experience. Even if we did not need this relapse into un-
consciousness after every eighteen hours or so for the sake
of physical rest we should still need it in order to divide
life up into manageable sections. Continuous consciousness
from the cradle to the grave, without regular pauses and
partial new beginnings, would be intolerable. The cease-
less bombardment of sense impressions, the unremitting engagement of the self with other people and with the circumstances and problems of our lives, would mount up to an
unbearable pressure. But in fact this pressure is relaxed
every night by the disengagement of sleep, making it possible to begin afresh in the morning. Of course the new
day offers only a relative beginning. The world has continued through the night, and yesterday's problems are
still there waiting to be taken up again. But nevertheless
the very fact of taking them up again offers the possibility of a varied approach. The new day opens up new possibilities. Time has passed; tension has been relaxed;
emotions have calmed; our mind has surveyed its problems
again and perhaps come to see them slightly differently.
And this continually repeated new beginning plays an important part in forming the structure and quality of our experience.

Now perhaps this effect of sleep in dividing our life
into parts which, having their own terminus, have each
their own shape and character, suggests an analogous function for death. Perhaps we are not ready for the endless
vista of eternal life because our life lacks that quality
which would alone make welcome the prospect of a limitless
future. But perhaps it is the function of mortality to
bracket a space within our immortal existence, making a
limited span within which to live. Within this horizon
there is the possibility of finite achievements and failures in finite situations, and consequently of the growth
and development of character.

This view involves both an attitude to life and an attitude to death. As regards the first, it means that we have a limited vista of life set before us, bounded by an end beyond which we cannot see; and upon this limited scene we have to concentrate all our thoughts and efforts. It is long enough for the greatest human plans and achievements, and yet short enough to give shape and urgency to life. Because time is limited it is precious. Because we do not live in this world for ever we have to get on with whatever we are going to do. Thus the attitude to life that follows from this view is in practice a this-worldly attitude involving a full concentration upon the affairs of the present life. And as regards our view of death, this is now related to the eternal life which consists in being eternally the object of God's love. Against this background, death will still always be faced with a profound awe and apprehension which engulfs our whole consciousness. But Christian faith seeks to match death as the totally unknown with a total trust in the love of God. Of course in fact this trust is usually far from total. It shares the wavering and fluctuating character of the believer's consciousness of God in the midst of his long pilgrimage. And accordingly the facing of death is often an ordeal of doubt and fear when for perfect faith it would have the different character of a great transition, coloured by the sadness of parting but not evoking deep dread or terror. We can only say that in so far as the trust is real and operative it must take the final sting out of death, the sting of ultimate meaninglessness and vacuity, and must thereby deprive the grave of its victory over life. There can be meaning and hope even in the moments prior to dissolution. And in the minds of those who are now left with an irreparable void in their lives there can be, mingled with their grief, the solemn thought of the trumpets that are sounding on the other side, and a sense of the loving sovereignty of God both here and beyond the dark mystery of death.

My suggestion, then, is that Christian thought is still committed to belief in a life after death; that there is no advantage in concealing this either from ourselves or from others; but that the Augustinian type of theology in which death is held to be the wages of sin should be replaced by an Irenaean type of theology which sees our mortality in relation to a positive divine purpose of love; and that ministry to the dying and to the bereaved, and the ceremonies of death and disposal, should so far as possible reflect this theological conception of death.

But, needless to say, I am well aware that every one of these theses is, to say the least, debatable; and I put them before you as material for debate.

Bibliography

The following works contain useful material for further study. The entry "(B)" signifies that the work listed contains an extensive bibliography.

A. *General Philosophical Works*

Broad, C. D., *The Mind and Its Place in Nature*. London: Routledge and Kegan Paul, 1937. Pp. 479–551.
Ducasse, C. J., *The Belief in a Life After Death*. Springfield, Ill.: Charles C. Thomas, 1961.
Flew, Antony, "Immortality," in *Encyclopedia of Philosophy*, Vol. 4, ed. Paul Edwards. New York: Macmillan, 1967. (B)
Flew, Antony (ed.), *Body, Mind and Death*. New York: Macmillan, 1964. (B)
Hick, John, *Biology and the Soul* (Arthur Stanley Eddington Memorial Lecture). Cambridge: Cambridge University Press, 1972.
MacIntyre, A. C., "A Note on Immortality," *Mind*, Vol. LXIV, 1955.
Martin, C. B., *Religious Belief*. Ithaca: Cornell University Press, 1959. Pp. 95–120.
Penelhum, Terence, *Religion and Rationality*. New York: Random House, 1971. Pp. 331–355.
Penelhum, Terence, *Survival and Disembodied Existence*. London: Routledge and Kegan Paul, 1970. (B)
Phillips, D. Z., *Death and Immortality*. London: Macmillan, 1970. (B)
Price, H. H., *Essays in the Philosophy of Religion*. Oxford: Clarendon Press, 1972.
Quinton, A. M., "The Soul," *Journal of Philosophy*, Vol. LIX, 1962.

Toynbee, Arnold, et al., *Man's Concern with Death*.   London:
    Hodder and Stoughton, 1968.
Williams, B.A.O., "Personal Identity and Individuation,"
    Proceedings of the Aristotelian Society, Vol. LVII,
    1956–1957.

B.   *The Platonic Doctrine of Immortality
     and its Predecessors*

Homer, *Odyssey*, Book XI.
Patterson, R. L., *Plato on Immortality*.   University Park,
    Pa.: The Pennsylvania State University Press, 1965.
Plato, *Phaedo, Phaedrus, Republic*.   Many editions are avail-
    able.   The best known are the collected translations
    of the Dialogues by Benjamin Jowett (Oxford), and the
    translations of the *Republic* by F. M. Cornford (Oxford)
    and A. D. Lindsay (Dutton: Everyman's Library).
Robinson, T. M., *Plato's Psychology*.   Toronto: University
    of Toronto Press, 1970.   (B)
Rohde, Erwin, *Psyche*.   London: Routledge and Kegan Paul,
    1925, 1950.

C.   *Doctrines of the Afterlife in Judaism,
     Christianity, and Islam*

Bell, Richard, *An Introduction to the Qur'an*.   Edinburgh:
    The University Press, 1953.
Brandon, S.G.F., *Man and His Destiny in the Great Religions*.
    Manchester: The University Press, 1962.   (B)
Brandon, S.G.F., *The Judgment of the Dead*.   London: Weiden-
    feld and Nicolson, 1967.   (B)
Charles, R. H., *Eschatology: The Doctrine of a Future Life
    in Israel, Judaism, and Christianity*.   New York: Schock-
    en Books, 1963 (originally published 1899, second edi-
    tion 1913).
Morison, Frank, *Who Moved the Stone?*   London: Faber and
    Faber, 1944.
Niebuhr, Richard R., *Resurrection and Historical Reason*.
    New York: Charles Scribner's Sons, 1957.
O'Shaughnessy, Thomas, *Muhammad's Thoughts on Death*.
    Leiden: E. J. Brill, 1969.
Olan, Levi A., *Judaism and Immortality*.   New York: Union
    of Hebrew Congregations, 1971.
Pelikan, Jaroslav, *The Shape of Death: Life, Death and Im-
    mortality in the Early Fathers*.   London: Macmillan,
    1962.

Perry, M. C., *The Easter Enigma*. London: Faber and Faber, 1959.

Ramsey, A. M., *The Resurrection of Christ*. London: Geoffrey Bles, 1945.

Robinson, J.A.T., *The Body: A Study in Pauline Theology*. London: S.C.M. Press, 1952.

Stendahl, K. (ed.), *Immortality and Resurrection*. New York: Macmillan, 1965.

Stewart, Roy A., *Rabbinic Theology*. Edinburgh: Oliver and Boyd, 1961.

Wolfson, H. A., "Immortality and Resurrection in the Philosophy of the Church Fathers," in *Religious Philosophy*. New York: Atheneum, 1965. Pp. 69–103. A response to Cullmann. Included in Stendahl.

D.   *Psychical Research and Survival*

Broad, C. D., *Lectures on Psychical Research*. London: Routledge and Kegan Paul, 1962.

James, William, *William James on Psychical Research*, ed. Murphy and Ballou. New York: Viking Press, 1960.

Murphy, Gardner, *Challenge of Psychical Research*. New York: Harper and Row, 1961.

Myers, F.W.H., *Human Personality and its Survival of Bodily Death*, abridged edition. London: Longmans, 1919.

Tyrrell, G.N.M., *The Personality of Man*. Harmondsworth: Pelican, 1946. (B)

See also the essays by Rosalind Heywood and H. H. Price in *Man's Concern with Death*, and several of the chapters in the volume by C. J. Ducasse. (Listed under A. above).

E.   *Secularization and Religious Belief*

Bultmann, Rudolf, "New Testament and Mythology," in H. W. Bartsch (ed.), *Kerygma and Myth*, trans. Fuller. London: S.P.C.K., 1953.

Mascall, E. L., *The Secularisation of Christianity*. London: Darton, Longman and Todd, 1965.

Pratt, Vernon, *Religion and Secularisation*. London: Macmillan, 1970. (B)

Robinson, J.A.T., *Honest to God*. London: S.C.M. Press, 1963.

van Buren, Paul M., *The Secular Meaning of the Gospel*. London: S.C.M. Press, 1963.

See also the volume by D. Z. Phillips listed under A. above.

F.   *Reincarnation*

Bouquet, A. C., *Hinduism*. London: Hutchinson, 1949.
Conze, Edward, *Buddhism*. London: Faber and Faber, 1957.
Deussen, Paul, *The Philosophy of the Upanishads*. New York:
    Dover, 1966.
Eliot, Sir Charles, *Hinduism and Buddhism*, 3 vols. London:
    Routledge and Kegan Paul, 1921.
Smart, Ninian, *Doctrine and Argument in Indian Philosophy*.
    London: Allen and Unwin, 1964.
Zaehner, R. C., *Hinduism*. London: Oxford University Press,
    1962.
See also Ninian Smart's contributions to *Man's Concern
    with Death* (A. above), and the relevant chapters of
    the two works (listed under C. above) by S.G.F. Brandon.

Basic Problems in Philosophy Series

A. I. Melden and Stanley Munsat
University of California, Irvine
General Editors

The Problem of Abortion
Joel Feinberg

Introduction   An Almost Absolute Value in History, *John T. Noonan, Jr.*   Abortion Decisions: Personal Morality, *Daniel Callahan*   Abortion and the Argument from Innocence, *Marvin Kohl*   Understanding the Abortion Argument, *Roger Wertheimer*   A Defense of Abortion and Infanticide, *Michael Tooley*   Abortion, Infanticide, and Respect for Persons, *S. I. Benn*   Abortion and the Sanctity of Human Life, *Baruch A. Brody*   A Defense of Abortion, *Judith Jarvis Thomson*   Abortion and the Law, *Baruch A. Brody*   Abortion Laws, *Daniel Callahan*   Williams v. State of New York   A Cause for "Wrongful Life": A Suggested Analysis, *Minnesota Law Review*   The 1973 Supreme Court Decisions on State Abortion Laws: Excerpts from Opinion in *Roe* v. *Wade*   Abortion: The New Ruling, *Hastings Center Report*   Bibliography

ETHICAL RELATIVISM
John Ladd

Introduction   Custom Is King, *Herodotus*   Ethics and Law: Eternal Truths, *Friedrich Engels*   Folkways, *William Graham Sumner*   The Meaning of Right, *W. D. Ross*   Ethical Relativity? *Karl Duncker*   Cultural Relativism and Cultural Values, *Melville J. Herskovits*   Ethical Relativity: Sic et Non, *Clyde Kluckhohn*   Social Science and Ethical Relativism, *Paul W. Taylor*   The Issue of Relativism, *John Ladd*   The Universally Human and the Culturally Variable, *Robert Redfield*   Bibliography

Human Rights
A. I. Melden

Introduction   The Second Treatise of Civil Government, Chapters 2 and 5, *John Locke*   Anarchical Fallacies, *Jeremy Bentham*   Natural Rights, *Margaret MacDonald*   Are There Any Natural Rights?, *H.L.A. Hart*   Justice and Equality, *Gregory Vlastos*   Rights, Human Rights, and Racial Discrimination, *Richard Wasserstrom*   Persons and Punishment, *Herbert Morris*   Appendices   Bibliography

Egoism and Altruism
Ronald D. Milo

Introduction   Self-Love and Society, *Thomas Hobbes*   Upon the Love of Our Neighbor, *Joseph Butler*   Morality, Self-Love, and Benevolence, *David Hume*   Morality and the Duty of Love toward Other Men, *Immanuel Kant*   Hedonism and Egoism, *Moritz Schlick*   Egoism as a Theory of Human Motives, *C. D. Broad*   An Empirical Basis for Psychological Egoism, *Michael A. Slote*   Altruistic Behavior, *Justin Aronfreed*   The Possibility of Altruism, *Thomas Nagel*   Bibliography

Guilt and Shame
Herbert Morris

Introduction   Stavrogin's Confession, *Fyodor Dostoyevsky*   Differentiation of German Guilt, *Karl Jaspers*   Origin of the Sense of Guilt, *Sigmund Freud*   Guilt and Guilt Feelings, *Martin Buber*   Real Guilt and Neurotic Guilt, *Herbert Fingarette*   "Guilt," "Bad Conscience," and the Like, *Friedrich Neitzsche*   The Sense of Justice, *John Rawls*   Shame, *Gerhart Piers* and *Milton B. Singer*   Autonomy v. Shame and Doubt, *Erik H. Erikson*   The Nature of Shame, *Helen Merrell Lynd*   Bibliography

The Analytic-Synthetic Distinction
Stanley Munsat

Introduction   First Truths, *Gottfried Wilhelm von Leibniz*   Necessary and Contingent Truths, *Gottfried Wilhelm von Leibniz*   Of Proposition, *Thomas Hobbes*   Introduction to the Critique of Pure Reason, *Immanuel Kant*   Kant, *Arthur Papp*   Of Demonstration, and Necessary Truths, *John Stuart Mill*   Views of Some Writers on the Nature of Arithmetical

Propositions, *Gottlob Frege*   What Is an Empirical Science? *Bertrand Russell*   Two Dogmas of Empiricism, *Willard Van Orman Quine*   The Meaning of a Word, *John Austin*   In Defense of a Dogma, *H. P. Grice* and *P. F. Strawson*   Bibliography

Civil Disobedience and Violence
Jeffrie G. Murphy

Introduction   On Disobeying the Law, *Socrates*   On the Duty of Civil Disobedience, *Henry David Thoreau*   Legal Obligation and the Duty of Fair Play, *John Rawls*   Social Protest and Civil Obedience, *Sydney Hook*   The Vietnam War and the Right of Resistance, *Jeffrie G. Murphy*   Civil Disobedience: Prerequisite for Democracy in Mass Society, *Christian Bay*   Non-violence, *Mohandas K. Gandhi*   A Fallacy on Law and Order: That Civil Disobedience Must Be Absolutely Nonviolent, *Howard Zinn*   On Not Prosecuting Civil Disobedience, *Ronald Dworkin*   Law and Authority, *Peter Kropotkin*   Bibliography

Punishment and Rehabilitation
Jeffrie G. Murphy

Introduction   People v. Levy, *California District Court of Appeals*   Punishment, *Stanley I. Benn*   The Right to Punish, *Immanuel Kant*   Persons and Punishment, *Herbert Morris*   Punishment and Utility, *Jeremy Bentham*   Punishment as a Practice, *John Rawls*   Capital Punishment, *Karl Marx*   Two Models of the Criminal Process, *Herbert L. Packer*   Criminal Psychodynamics: A Platform, *Benjamin Karpman*   Therapy, Not Punishment, *Karl Menninger*   Punishment, *B. F. Skinner*   A Preventive System of Criminal Law, *Barbara Wootton*   Criminal Justice, Legal Values, and the Rehabilitative Ideal, *Francis A. Allen*   The Myth of Mental Illness, *Thomas S. Szasz*   Criminal Punishment and Psychiatric Fallacies, *Jeffrie G. Murphy*   Preventive Detention and Psychiatry, *Jeffrie G. Murphy*   Crime, Clutchability, and Individuated Treatment, *Joel Feinberg*   Appendix on Psychosurgery, *Jeffrie G. Murphy*   Bibliography

Immortality
Terence Penelhum

Introduction   Immortality, *Peter Geach*   Survival and the Idea of "Another World," *H. H. Price*   The Resurrection of

Christ and the Resurrection of Men, *St. Paul* Immortality
of the Soul or Resurrection of the Dead?, *Oscar Cullmann*
from "Theology and Verification," *John Hick* The Resurrection: Objections and Answers, *St. Thomas Aquinas* The
Problem of Life After Death, *H. H. Price* The Question of
Survival, *Antony Flew* Towards a Christian Theology of
Death, *John Hick* Bibliography

Morality and the Law
Richard A. Wasserstrom

Introduction On Liberty, *John Stuart Mill* Morals and
the Criminal Law, *Lord Patrick Devlin* Immorality and
Treason, *H.L.A. Hart* Lord Devlin and the Enforcement of
Morals, *Ronald Dworkin* Sins and Crimes, *A. R. Louch*
Morals Offenses and the Model Penal Code, *Louis B. Schwartz*
Paternalism, *Gerald Dworkin* Four cases involving the en-
forcement of morality Bibliography

War and Morality
Richard A. Wasserstrom

Introduction The Moral Equivalent of War, *William James*
The Morality of Obliteration Bombing, *John C. Ford, S.J.*
War and Murder, *Elizabeth Anscombe* Moral Judgment in Time
of War, *Michael Walzer* Pacifism: A Philosophical Analysis,
Jan Narveson On the Morality of War: A Preliminary In-
quiry, *Richard Wasserstrom* Judgment and Opinion, The In-
ternational Tribunal, Nuremberg, Germany Superior Orders,
Nuclear Warfare, and the Dictates of Conscience, *Guenter
Lewy* Selected Bibliography